LADY
BUSINESS

A Celebration of Lesbian Poetry

ALEXANDER, ARKANSAS
WWW.SIBLINGRIVALRYPRESS.COM

Lady Business: A Celebration of Lesbian Poetry

ISBN: 978-1-937420-18-5
Bryan Borland, Editor
Philip F. Clark, Art Editor
Copyright © 2012 by Sibling Rivalry Press

Cover Art: "Vessel Reflection" by Bil Donovan. Used by Permission.

Sibling Rivalry Press, LLC
13913 Magnolia Glen Drive
Alexander, AR 72002

www.siblingrivalrypress.com
info@siblingrivalrypress.com

First Sibling Rivalry Press Edition: August 2012

LADY BUSINESS

SALLY BELLEROSE

PERFECT FUTURE

SALLY BELLEROSE is author of *The Girls Club* (Bywater Books, September 2011). She was awarded a Fellowship in Literature from the National Endowment for the Arts based on an excerpt from this novel. The manuscript won the Bywater Prize for Fiction and was a finalist for the James Jones Fellowship, the Thomas Wolfe Fiction Prize, and the Bellwether Endowment. Sally is also a poet who loves rhythm, story, and language. Her poems and prose usually involve themes of sexuality, illness, and class. In writing, she is interested in messy, confusing, complicated relationships. She is also drawn to humor and transcendence. She has published one volume of poetry titled *Sex Crimes*. Her poems have appeared in numerous and diverse publications ranging from a text book titled *A Call to Nursing* to *Boston Literary Review*, and poems here have previously appeared in *Spilling Ink, Handful of Dust, Sojourner: A Feminist Anthology, Alternatives to Surrender, Broad River Review, The Poetry of Sex, Women on Women 2, My Lover is a Woman, Best Bisexual Erotica, Shape of a Box*, and *Naugatuck River Review*.

sallybellerose.wordpress.com

MARRIED LADIES HAVE SEX IN THE BATHROOM

We did it everywhere.
We were middle-aged women
with middle-aged husbands
and school-aged children.

Mostly in daylight.
Mostly in twenty minutes
or less.
In places so common
they'd never suspect.

Every room of both houses,
the cellar,
the garage,
the neighbors' children's four-foot wading pool.

And then there were the bathrooms,
the bathrooms,
the bathrooms of Fitzwillies,
                    the GirlsClub,
                        Caldor's,
                            Shoprite,
                    the bushes
in back of the bar at the end of the street.

We did it on my picnic table,
and under her picnic table.
We did it in extremes,
dressed for inclement weather.

Coming, fully clothed,
hats,
scarves,
boots,
and mittens.

Coming, buck screaming naked,
in the hot dirt,
of some God forsaken road,
with bugs crawling,
in woods that never gave back
her pink lace panties.

We did it lying flat
on the kitchen floor,
our heads pressing up against the kitchen door.
Our bodies barring our boys' entrance.

We did it seated
in my car, moving,
in her car, in the body shop,
at the airport,
on the plane to Baltimore
while she calmly discussed
Women, War, and Peace
with another woman in the next seat.

In the hot tubs,
even though I hate the hot tubs.
On the stairs outside the hot tubs,
not waiting for the couple inside
to come out.

We did it with phones ringing,
kids screaming,
dogs barking,
tubs overflowing,
and dinner burning in the pot.
We did it with fingers so hot
we thought for sure we'd be branded forever.

We did it with bodies so tired,
hearts so heavy,
that doin it was the last thing
on our minds.
Still, something greedy whispered,
get it while you can girls,
because you never know
if or when
you're gonna get again.

We did it and called it empowerment,
lust,
avarice,
and adultery.
We dared man or nature
to deny that doin it
was anything but sacred.

We flaunted.
We hid.
Tense and tangled,
sometimes we forgot
when to run, when to taunt.

We stopped.
Caught our breaths, confronted.
Like dogs in heat, we fought.
Our lives uprooted,
recovered to fight,
to blame some more.

In the end
we cared for ourselves
enough to stay
alive, in this world, together.

And a year,
and a year,
and the years go by.
Less and less
we press each other.

Still we love.
But oh the sex.
It's never been the same.
Life on the edge is an addiction.
Honest life is pleasant,
better, definitely better,
but so damned tame.

LILY PAD

This poem is no haiku
It's a fantasy
of frog-thighed lovers
hopping on
hopping off

Ker-plunk
and gone

No mamsy pamsy
Sorry about the wet skin
and webbed feet
May I ma'am's
for me

LILY PAD: HAIKU QUICKIE

Frog-thighed lover.   Hopped on.   Kerplunk.   Gone.

AGING

When there's nothing left in the garden but garlic, parsnip, and tomatoes that may or may not withstand the predicted light frost, I compete with squirrels for grounded butternuts. The flesh around the woody shell is green and fuzzy. My fingers are tarry with the handling. In a month, left in our dry cellar, with luck, the fuzzy flesh will become brittle husks, but the meat inside will remain moist and fit to be eaten. The shell is similar to a walnut, but thicker and harder. By November if the nuts don't rot, the mice don't find them, and if there is no snow, I will take a hammer to the shell, on the sidewalk, like I did as a kid. Maybe one in ten will be "just right" with a toasty flavor. To most palates the butternut is not as pleasant as the walnut, its better-known cousin. Nine in ten will be either "under" with an astringent taste or "over" with a slightly rotten dirty taste. Nine in ten will either never reach my mouth or get spit in the yellowing grass. But the meat of that one in ten will be the perfect combination of oily texture and slightly bitter taste that make the foraging worthwhile. The best part is tossing the shells in a bucket, the satisfying lonely thump in the ear that only a child, or an adult remembering the smug secrets of that child exiled to the side yard for bad behavior, competing with squirrels for grounded butternuts, ever gets to hear.

DEAR EMILY

Agreed / there is verse / worthy of reflection / in the buzz / of every being

BYE BYE BARBARA

She went slowly,
with very little meat
between the skin
and spine.

Still,
until the end
she tried
to make a straight line
of bone.

Hungry all the time.

The big surprise was her eyes,
how they bulged
with the world
getting bigger in her orbits
as she died.

RUMORS

Geese circling, raucous
leave-taking,
v forming and fading from view.
You lean on your hoe
listening as their voices recede to one,
softer, sadder as they go.
The flock taking something of you with them
as you follow that last rumor of sound,
the honking that mocks and makes beautiful your loneliness.

SISTERS, WAITING

My beloved sister, baby sister, tell-her-everything sister sits next to me on a row of plastic chairs pressed together in the waiting room outside Intensive Care. It's midnight. We're talked out. Nodding at my purse, which hangs from the back of my chair, she quotes Mom, "Put that on your lap."

"Hand through the strap." I complete the advice and comply.

Our eyelids close.   Open.   Close.

She sleeps or does something like sleep. I sleep or do something like sleep. Two middle-aged sisters, nodding on chairs, waiting to see where Daddy goes this time, slouched toward each other, crowns touching, resting head to head, conjoined twins with poor prognosis for future separation.

We sleep, but even in sleep, the conversation seeps through scalp and skull, bone and skin, just temporal pulsing, easy as heartbeat, until her blood whispers, "Where do they really go, the grateful dead?" Open as a baby sister, too new to know big sister doesn't have a clue.

I twitch. We bump heads. Our purses fall. Their big mouths open. Her cell phone blinks and rings, one false ring, before it skitters toward the snack machine. We pick combs, wallets, pads, and pens from the floor. Not knowing what to pray for, we sit up and stare straight ahead, wondering how much longer, Daddy?

Not quite believing or disbelieving what our father has taught us about life after death, we take our waking slowly. A soft-soled nurse approaches calling our family name.

We hold our father's hands, and say, "We love you, Daddy." His answer is a death rattle. After his breathing stops and starts and stops, never to start again, my middle-aged baby sister takes my hand and I understand it's not so much answers she longs for as the promise that conversation will not end.

DEMENTIA WINE

Days turned night side up,
he is nonetheless awake, his nose flat
against the window pane this morning.
His spouse says, "Eat your breakfast, darling."
"Front row seat." He nods. "Look,
our backyard is Broadway."

Sleep deprived by his night wanderings,
his spouse squints out a dirty window,
sees his chorus line of berries
dewed in glamour on the leggy vines.

With coffee and Fibre O's
from the breakfast nook they follow
the day warming to full rehearsal,
berries high stepping in the heat,
plumped in longing,
keeping perfect time.

"Dying to be picked and eaten,"
he sings portly sweet,
waving from the window,
"Red raspberry... black raspberry
choose me... choose me."
He's in a good mood.
His meds are working.

By late morning he is dozing on the Lazy Boy.
His spouse is drinking yet another cup of coffee,
staring at low-hung,
fermenting berries,
dangling in the hot sun.

All is quiet then, except one Jay
caws and staggers.
It's too early, even for a matinee.
How they had loved the theater.

The spouse watches.
Delighted by the bad bird's
peck peck pecking,
he wakes his husband.

"Come, come see your Broadway,
there's a villain with a beak-full,
badgering the chorus
getting drunk on stolen wine."

PEPERE

Pepere is too big for the box. He doesn't smell like Pepere. He smells like pine and powder. His skin is pulled too tight, too white on his face. A starched shirt stretches across his belly. I stare at him, lying in his box in the living room. When they left him alone on the feather bed he looked like Pepere. Memere comes to stand behind me. Before I can ask where Pepere will go in his small box, she puts her hand on my shoulder and says, "Come away then, Poche Molle." That's what Pepere calls me, Poche Molle, because I have fat cheeks, like him. She says, "Come away then, Poche Molle," but stands still as a tree with her hand on my shoulder, staring at Pepere. The rest of the grown-ups and kids are at the other house, my house next door, getting dressed in their best clothes. That's what you do when someone dies. But Memere is still in her house dress and I am still in my play clothes. Soft, like a secret, Memere says, "They should have let him be." The back door creaks. Memere takes her hand off my shoulder. "Come away then, Poche Molle." I don't want to leave him, but I have to get dressed in my best clothes.

DANCING

She is three-feet tall and she is dancing.
She is singing, "Jingle bells. I have a little dreidel,"
and she is dancing.

Her twin brother Mikey has been dying.
He is four days dead. She is three years old
and she is dancing.

She weighs thirty pounds
and she is spinning. She is twirling
on the dance floor in the Garden House
rented for Mikey's after-funeral meal.

Friends and family are sitting at round tables
watching or not watching
as she is slowing. She is stopping.
She is bowing to her auntie,
asking for this dance.

She is rising in her auntie's arms,
circling skinny legs
around her auntie's waist.
They are waltzing on parquet.

She is laughing, "Faster, Auntie, faster,"
calling, "Mikey, Mikey, Mikey,"
singing, "Jingle all the way."

She is saying, "Put me down,"
wheeling round the dance floor,
looking back and laughing,
"Chase me, Auntie, chase me."

Friends and family are eating
ham and tuna,
exhausting conversation,
"He is going to a better place,
resting with the Lord."

She is hopping. She is stomping,
kicking off a shoe.
She is sitting on the floor,

talking to patent leather,
naming her right shoe Mikey,
saying, "Mikey," as she slips him on,
"You can't talk to me any more."
She is up and she is dancing.

SPIN

The Poem is the Hummer carrying
bottled water and weapons
to the war zone.

The Poem is the channel,
tread, and the spin of a tire,
the gravel that spit on the child
abandoned on the side of the road.

The Poem, of course, is the child.

BRIT BLALOCK

My Mother Made Me Wear This Dress

BRIT BLALOCK recently completed her MFA in poetry at New York University. Her work has previously appeared or is forthcoming in *Booth*, *Blood Orange Review*, Argos Books' *Little Anthology*, and more. Blalock is originally from the Alabama gulf coast.

SUNDAY SCHOOL, BEFORE COFFEE AND DONUTS

My mother made me wear this dress.
You're nearly eleven and too borrowed.

I should never wear low necklines.
Adults are throwing knives that just miss.

Halloween is for the devil.
They do not know about the knife throwing, maybe.

Solomon threatened to cut a baby in half, but it didn't happen.
You haven't been baptized in anything so far, not even spite.

I know all the books of the Bible.
There are three things you still don't know.

Water can ruin lives,
one day you'll love a woman,

you're not the only one who loses Jesus
in your own backyard.

HOMETOWN GIRL

it was a different year a better
smile like glass and chimes without
the knees we wore the same blue
rings like mermaids I think it was or ribbons
should I know the street we read the signs
and changed the letters because minutes were still
little lines and didn't we walk didn't we
go somewhere around the block

*

she had the camera for a sash it was lighter
than skin or a lampshade hat my mother did
everything best shh the Olympics are on
I could have been a runner slow down she said
I'm not that way I'm just telling you
something much like words

*

the pressure that our breasts were giving
underneath that air we broke into pieces
like whisks it made me gag the swiftness
there is butter somewhere understand
I could have made you take
a bite we could hold hands you know

*

I am hanging things on walls she had empty
cans there twenty-four sound of hand to mouth
you're a mess we're not baking pies
with those things on our hands
what are those things

MISE-EN-SCÈNE

It was raining hats yesterday. Charlie and I just stood outside and caught them in nets. Cowboy hats, baseball caps, sombreros. They floated down slowly, like handkerchiefs. We were in a movie without a title. I yelled for someone to stop the hats, but the shot kept rolling. A voice said, *This scene cost us a million dollars, so don't fuck it up.* Then music started playing. It was sort of jazzy and all wrong. I took Charlie's hand without meaning to, and the hats stopped. She whispered, *Walk towards the camera, but don't look at it.* The light began to change: I had never seen a sun-less sunset.

RUTH 5:1-8

[1]Ruth often left the bed of Boaz in the hollow of the night. His arm fell too harshly against her eggshell ribs. [2]Hours before the sun began to slope, she would flee to the room where Naomi slept, holding Ruth's son like a relic. [3]The three of them rested quietly until hearing the sound of men threshing grain in a nearby room.

[4]One morning, faces an inch apart, Ruth petitioned, "Let us leave this place. We can return to Moab with Obed, and I will beg in the fields there."

[5]Naomi closed her eyes and thought of the famine, replied apologetically, "We will never know hunger here."

[6]Weeks later, Boaz discovered Ruth leaving his room in the dream hours. He discouraged her seven times with a whip. [7]Before morning, Naomi took to dressing Ruth's wounds; her thin fingers eased the plowed skin with ointment. [8]Ruth wept without moving. Naomi counted her eyelashes, kissed the corners of her mouth, brought her something to eat.

I WAS THINKING WE SHOULD GET NAKED

and throw the leftovers out. Maybe
these machine words will stop
slinking up, quit climbing in our mouths

and making homes without doors.
Instead, we've swabbed everything
with alcohol, so sure that the sting

brings life back. Meanwhile, past
loves stay stuck— old vinyl
on sweaty thighs. *Mon petit artichaut,*

peel them away, so I can find
your green heart.

WHY BISEXUAL IS A DIRTY WORD
OR
MY MOTHER TELLS ME TO PUT DOWN MY TORCH, SO I WRITE
THIS POEM INSTEAD.
for Bernard

Let someone else do
the shouting, she says—
my mother who does nothing
if she doesn't do
some shouting and high-heel
to ground stomping.

I mumble something back
about the gay rights movement
looking like the civil rights
movement but pause
to wonder if that's offensive
because I was born into this
milk-skin that I never stopped
to thank anyone for.

My thoughts turn to my little brother
who has a parent of each
color (black and white, I mean),
but everyone's been telling him
he's black since day one
except he was raised in my family
which truth be told
ain't black at all.

So now I'm back to the word
bisexual and what it must mean
to be stuck in the middle;
I think my brother must know
as much about it as I do
especially since we both have
a Mom from a generation
that wants everybody to pick
a damn team.

Who, one day when I came
to her with my queer

and stalling heart, told me
bisexual is what people call
themselves when they can't
claim the word gay.

While I want to be angry,
somehow I am grateful
that she at least believes
it's OK to be a gay person
because I have friends
who still aren't allowed
at Christmas dinner
because their parents
think Jesus will smite them
right there at the table
as someone's passing
the cornbread or sweet tea.

Just thinking the word
Jesus makes me feel guilty,
like I've abandoned the other
queer kids in the South
by fleeing to New York;
I picture them at church camp
together, petitioning god
with actual sincerity to take
the big gay cross away.

Mom continues her argument
saying, *It's not like there's even*
a radical act left for you,
which sounds like the hippie
generation prattling, as if
they invented the word *protest.*

I say, *Can gay people*
get married yet?
And the answer is clear,
but she seems to think
the wait won't be too long
which really gets me
riled up and I scream,
Shouldn't I be allowed
to marry whoever I want?

So now we've come right
back to her point about
me having to be the one
doing all the shouting,
which I do, so while she takes
the next few months to decide
whether she'll leave my father
or let him stay
in their bed, I pick my torch
back up and let it burn
my own fucking hand
just to be sure
I can still catch fire.

CASSANDRA CHRISTENSON

FIRE FINGERS

CASSANDRA CHRISTENSON's work has been published in *My Life Is Poetry*, *E-33*, *Writings from Emeritus* and *The Chronicles*. As a registered nurse, Cassandra founded Project Nightlight for those alone and nearing the end of life. She is 76, has a 50-year-old daughter, and is grateful to have come out as an older person after a turbulent life trying to be something she was not. She finds liberation in being herself.

HOW POETRY CAME INTO MY LIFE

Late October of my life poetry waited
long until I a fertile field ready for plowing
yet again before the frost.

Poetry fierce in deep folds of far mountains
holds breath until I lie myself down
sink into earth ready willing for seeding
before winter.

Then poetry rolls into thunder. Lightning stabs
blank book, thrusts pen to my hand.
Storm blows as force to lift high, me up out
of muck to ride great winds, tsunami of words.

My song long hidden, denied until I lay myself
down in fields to lie fallow. Wait into yielding.
Allow rotting; the wilting.

'Til spring called forth to move into world of word,
ink to pour out of my veins, rip open page and weep
into paper, tear up my soul, ignite the healing.

I shout yes to beat, melody of words, harmony of music
and poetry to tame wildness until
it does not.

Then again to lie down in earth
to die.

Until yet another spring.

UNCLAIMED MEMORIES OF MY FATHER

ONE
My Father's Shadow

I am a flame thrower, a starving dog gnashing
on by father's shadow, his flesh yet in my teeth,
to tear away the pain. Things I do not know
wrench my mind as sign language struggles to
be deciphered of mewing, bleating child. Wisps
of father upon farthest wall where finger nails
drag deep sliding down through stone, blood red
scars unreadable to all.

I wrench neck of dragon, leap upon its back,
shout, "Keeper of Darkest Secrets, I ride your roar
into my past, suck fire that I may know the truth."
        "Did it happen?"

But baggage lies still against the farthest wall,
unclaimed, passengers gone home as baby girl
in basket floats decades all alone, I come to grab
her from the river, raise her high upon the
thrusting heaving beast as we ride into the sea
throw net out across the waters, call up shards
of me and him, the Daddy that I love, lost fathoms
far below where memory lies as death, waiting on
ocean's darkest floor.

UNCLAIMED MEMORIES OF MY FATHER

TWO
My Father: An Upright Man

The noble man, man of the community, scout leader,
teacher, Deacon of the church. I don't remember his
cotton shirts; they must have been white and pressed
by whom I do not know. I do remember the faded grey
stripes on thin cotton of boxer shorts lying loose over
golden hairs and skin color of fresh skinned bone.

On Saturdays I press those shorts
across steamy padded board, push hard the iron
into puckery part of rear then side panels and
finally the fly. I smooth his laundered socks, roll
them into a ball place in neat rows in heavy oak,
bottom drawer. He wears socks held high upon
his leg, garter and strap firm in place. I do not
know pattern or color of tie but I see the way he loops
it about around his neck tucks into smooth hard
knot and lays the tails smooth and firm down
his chest just so.

Like how he lays me down upon his bed, a birthday
gift at 18, I suppose, touches my breast because,
because? I do not know nor do I wish. I jumped up
and ran and running since with glee in winds no
longer blow, pretty little girl voice of someone I
do not know for to strangle all is known.

I do remember that moment, blue and purple afghan,
dormer window looking to roses bent over and grey,
and I am grateful for that spot of clear knowing so
perhaps the rest is true, but just lost now begging,
loud for words.

UNCLAIMED MEMORIES OF MY FATHER

THREE
The Story I Do Not Know

The moon closes behind the storm the night my father
comes. He marches into the dark. Tickly, Prickly is he,
presses in hard my cheek and chin, "I am going to come
and get you," a laughter I have never heard. Window
trappings shiver, fluttery winds of shame as Mr. Whiskers
grabs up my life to keep his

     Hounds at bay.

My face burns heat then pain. He says "Little Rosebud"
calls my lips to come and make it all so much better
and take the pain away. It is Little Rosebud's fault
and tells me I, as a little child, am colder than a fish.

     He says more but I am far away.

Now strike the banner, flail the staff, ram it high,
thrash the wind to the sun god. As I child-bride
married to the King to gather fruit in orchard of
his dead and dying manhood.

UNCLAIMED MEMORIES OF MY FATHER

FOUR
The Secreted Transfigured

I count on one hand and then on two, and on and
on, days until my life will be mine again, the life
I hope to live, my servitude lived out. But time
goes on as unclaimed memory pulls long upon
my soul til lightning strikes, ignites the loss,
bonfire leaps from fathoms deep and scratches
out the sky, to release its twisted hidden form into
                    rolling exploding rage.

GAZING INTO WINTER

I stand in my backyard garden
in fading hours of fall
gazing over fence at winter.
Pale sun warms my arms and face,
earth solid and friendly below my feet.
I see last of summer blossoms aglow but
it is no longer flowers I pick and strew for beauty.
It is winter vegetables to harvest
as I wait for spring to plant again.

When first freeze strikes distant hills
the Goddess comes awaits with me
stands with a certain kind of knowing
and is all around and within
as my mother, father and my lover
wraps lush robe about me to lead me through
frost and then the winter as I shudder
into her arms lay my head upon her breast
I am her own, my heart bursting walls that separate.
Our blood blends.

She swims marrow of my being, shining
showering me with dazzle to encourage
and in the midst of laughter
I wake into spring.

WHO WRITES IN ME

Know me, weaver, teller of story.
I am dancer, dances upon page
spinning life into song, melody flowing
rivers of lives, spreading secrets like honey
smooth onto paper.

I am the One, voice for the many who show up,
strumming of psyche, call of hidden,
wild place of the soul, waiting for telling.

So to you, heathen, grab lightning,
stab the dark. Pick up pen, lute or harp,
stride into winter, follow the thread,
bed down in snow. Slow telling of story
long simmering of heart.

Give birth to knowing, hatching the egg,
grabbing the gut, bleeding into pain,
jugular of truth with Me, teller of story.

I say "Yes," pour out your song, all your
laughter to strings or rattle, your fingers to drum
feet to floor, give voice to the dark.

Join gatherings round fire through eons of time
in lair and den, on past through the dawn

to depths of ones being, bring pen to book
set page afire, dance your story into flight.

For there I am ablaze
roaring;
The Teller of Truth

SUMMER BEFORE SNOW

She dances like fire and smiles secrets I do not know.
Turquoise shirt tight to body, Levi's, scuffed boots,
I feel moist, somewhere never felt before.

Square dance packed. Ponies run wild right off
carousel and I, familiar with birthday parties and
grammar school graduation, peek a moment out
of small town isolation toward womanhood with
razzle-dazzle of college kids up for summer work
in deep forest of Sierras play for "keepers."

She walks me home to my father, campsite in cool,
dense pines. Laughing college lady asks, "How old are you?"
with eyes as Hedy Lamar simmering in *Samson and Delilah.*
"Almost 16." 16 no, flash in my brain, but 14 and fluttery
duckling wanting to play big girl in thin air of high mountains.

Quick the invitation to next night party. She from
Fresno State rah rah with her crowd going crazy
and relief. Doors slam us in. 4 door Pontiac,
her hand like my father's to back of my head, fingers
in my hair, holds my face tight to angora and breast
gone firm, my nose into warm, pink fluff, smell of Ivory
and trace of sweat.

Car carves mountain's sharp shoulders with road,
road holding on, its edge teetering above long fall
to Three Rivers. Almost miss turn onto dirt where
car claims us and as forest closes in. Windows blur,
car slightly off kilter and headlights shoot deep
through trees where night things quick stir.

Now from far distant hills of 6 decades hence I stare
into tangle of memories fondle with mitten-ed fingers
sorting out meaning of long gone time ago of
Miss Bear Woman on edge and hungry for warm as
her lips scurry about the soft parts of my neck, sucking
gentle as young one on up to pink shell of my ear open
to entering, her tongue no parent could warn of. I felt heat.
Something unknown, yielding and wanting where wetness
waited. Never felt before and not ever again.

We come to the meadow. Army blankets spread,
laid down in moist grasses, beer poured, bodies
and clothes pressing, flash lights lying still
pointing into dark.

She lifts me up, tricks glint in her eyes, hand against
my back we fall into shadows, laughter left behind.
Night scampers stop, whiskers a tremble as Moon
holds her breath, alone in the night.

Winter comes early as snow drifts on still life and
somewhere in night the river freezes over and
silver fish slow.

NIGHT IN SIERRAS

Long time ago before silver there was
green spring of my life when nights
were filled with music and the fragrance
of pine and campfires

fire fingers clicked tart lemon air
bleeding out sorrow of slender souls.

We sang long, sat til cold, doused
fire, watched thunderheads of stars
rumble night sky as great dragon
forest breathed, slow switched its
tail, half crawled our spines.

We shuddered, left steamy embers,
to crawl into the belly of our sleeping bags
        And we smile.

I AM OLD

Yes, you tell me
when I stand in line
pretty woman behind me
you take first

Yes, you tell me
when I ask something
and your flat eyes look beyond

When I smile and flirt
"good morning" on Venice beach
natural thing for me
you say "old woman"
as if end of spit
taste of bitter melon
fresh in your mouth

I sit inside myself
same as when I am six
full of sunshine silliness
and waiting to grow up
now in deep glow of fall
I thread lightly
into time of the snows

I cannot escape my body
in its waning time
it falters on the stairs
pushes hard to take the next
flight up, lifting, dragging
wet laundry, jugs of life
bags of old letters

I will not fall down
far
but raise myself up
to dance
the last lingering waltz of myself
to take up the thread and weave
write my life
mend frayed edges
and begin
yet again

Planting time is not over
new season begun
time has crowned me
with gift of wings
unfolding in birthing wetness

I stretch tall, move wide
winging into richness
write my clearest
dance my wildness
speak a song

New fruits
trees to leave
grow to goodness

Gold is in harvest
of this moment
until I explode

And become
the laughter

FIRE RAGE

November 6, 1961.
   Bel Air
   hills burning
   houses
   animals

I don't want to go to therapy
   tell her I started it
   I know I did not
   but in a way I did
      Must confess.

482 homes on crest of Bel Air
   sparking, igniting, burning
   and what burned inside me
   so strong it could ignite fires
   all the way to Burma.

Flames of who I am and am not
   and who I am supposed to be.

I remember standing at summer party
   in kitchen over white enamel stove
   pregnant and wanting to stuff bra
   with Kleenex. Set it aflame just above
   seven month old unborn child
   I want to be incendiary
      Torch my self.

Where's the gasoline
   kerosene
   burn baby, burn
   burn away the evidence of woman
   burn away the breast, milk
   the need, wanting,
     The yearning

Turn it all into charcoal
     Kill Kill Kill

I am a cow udder full to bursting
    take to slaughter empty carcass
        Dying
        Dead

I want it all to go
    the woman part to go
    the yielding
    loving in the face of accepting
    accepting of who I am.

In the face of knowing
    knowing who I am
    knowing the truth of me
    under the embers
    simmering
        The Truth.

MARTY CORREIA

NOT A MANGO

MARTY CORREIA is a fiction- and poetry-writing lesbian husband living in the East Village with arts activist Kate Conroy, her spouse of 15 years. Her work has appeared in small literary journals and she has read at Bluestockings Bookstore and Dixon Place. Studying fiction at NYU's MFA program in Creative Writing, Marty is writing a novel about three generations of magicians from Bridgeport, Connecticut.

THE LAST(ING)

In a valley of pleasure
You took it in, stuck it out, pulled it on, shot it up
Flesh leather red, needle blue

A church with no roof
Rimbaud on a cross
No cloth, only loin

Puritans crushed
Prudence reviled
Drawn penises photographed

Dancing barefoot
She whirled around you
Lifted you up, she lifts you up

From the street, from the bed
Refusing your time to pass away
You were just kids along with the disease

Proud of your dust
Queer predecessors wash, rinse, repeat
Bathing in your scripture

Yet, today, nannies mind babies
And microwave Fresh Direct
Where you gave head

Next to your empty deathbed
Girly boy boas are flattened under
Books of criticism and theory

They don't know the Bowery
Still hears your heels clicking
Just yesterday, some bricks on Bond
Said they miss your shadow
And there are still some freaks left
Who would snort your ashes

NO WIRE HANGERS

Your drink was Malibu.
Your convertible, a LeBaron.
Your movie, Mommy Dearest.
Your dance, Vogue.

We were an odd couple.
High school dropout sweethearts.
You had a dancer's stance and graceful arms
and my jacket always hung on you like a father's.

A hot young manboy,
you were wasted on this boydyke.
I didn't deserve you
spending late nights
posing on the shredding white '70s
wicker furniture in the motel office
where I worked
the night desk. Where you entertained
me.

The '50s motel brought out your Vegas
and I think I hear a bell ding
when I evoke your smile's glint.

You did a strip tease
next to the coffee machine.
Maybe I could remember that night better
but you did stuff
that powdered cake donut
down your tighty whities.

Were we that lonely?
We were a couple
who didn't need to talk.
But our teeth chattered
at the February Atlantic
when you took my arm
as we strolled
an abandoned Herring Cove.

Were we that alone?
We drove 45 miles

to that empty beach
just to be where we belonged,
breathing in crisp queer air.
(Yes, we have our own air.)

It took twenty years,
but last night
I missed you.
It was how the songstress sounded,
it was what she sang... an Essex Hemphill poem
and it was why.
The queen had poise
and her voice...
Her voice made me turn to my left
to share a look with you,
to say
"Up there and under lights,
one of us. We have arrived.
We are not alone."

Could that be the first moment
I've missed you?
I turned my head
to share a look with you,
but you were gone.
You've been gone
so long.

Your death was AIDS. *lover died*
Your drink, Malibu.
Your convertible, a LeBaron.
Your movie, Mommy Dearest.
Your dance, Vogue.

A TRANSUBSTANTIAL FANTASY

*Inspired by "My Sweet Lord," an anatomically correct milk chocolate sculpture
of Jesus Christ by artist Cosimo Cavallaro*

Maybe it's the theobroma cacao talking,
but the usual Eucharist fails to feed my soul.

Barry White sings
Your Sweetness is My Weakness
and you rise to tell this disciple,
"This is my body, this *is* my body."

Your ashy skin begs for cocoa butter.
Starting at your feet, I massage you to luster.
Working my way to your face, I see it in your eyes,
a longing for a brush of Mary Magdalene's hair on your chest.

After our mouths mingle, you say I taste like vanilla
and I get the joke, because this fantasy is perfect.
But in real life, I would not hear your voice
over the one in my head saying, "Wow, Jesus can *kiss*."

Marty Correia

A ROSE IS A ROSE IS A... A METAPHOR
A response to "Lesbian Poetry"

She refuses to be a juicy mess
or fruit or mollusk under a dress.

This private part almost refused to be in this poem
but lost patience with the women, wimmin, womyn —
reciting odes to labia,
plums that throb, wait, rush, gush.

In pinks and reds,
                    on the beach,
                                    in the dark,
wet and ready.

No one writes of a vagina on a bus.
Or at a funeral,
still and dry.

Why don't Sapphic bards
leave the juicy
peach whole,
dangling from a branch?

In solidarity with all mother earth's vulvas,
please refuse all metaphors.

My cunt is not a mango.

AT THE SYNAGOGUE

Inspired by "In the Waiting Room" by Elizabeth Bishop

In Worcester, Massachusetts
I went with my father
to his job at the synagogue
where I mopped floors
and dusted books.
It was late fall. The sun set
early. The building empty
except for Rabbi Mendel,
a dark long overcoat and brimmed black hat.
My father vacuumed the basement
after a bar mitzvah
and two flights above him
I dusted books, piling
them in a cabinet.

The writing on the spines
looked upside down
or carved, but any way I held
them, I could not read it.
I guessed at what
the squiggles told
my father's employers:
Wear your yarmulke, pray
every day, don't turn on
your stove on Saturday.

Rabbi Mendel handed my father cash
and touched the back of my head to say:
Abel, you are lucky
to have such a good boy.

My father gave a Dad wink
that said to say nothing.
I thanked him and again went to work
at the back of the empty synagogue.
I continued to dust the books,
while I sat in the men's section.
At their services the women
and men were separated
by a glass partition.

Time passed. Rabbi Mendel walked in
shaking his head. But didn't he just
call me a boy? A good boy?
I said to myself:
You are one of them
and he knows.

His pant legs, tall black columns
topped with cotton string pigtails blocked me in.
The Torah listened from its haven but
windows proved the sky
had not darkened with holy clouds.

When Rabbi Mendel said:
Never put the siddurim on the floor.
I started crying: Sorry.
He said: You are a good boy.
You did not know.

He took my hand
and put a quarter in my palm.
Leaving me, he said something
in the language of his books.

It was time to leave and
in the basement, my father
told me to wrap up party leftovers.
I wrapped the broken kuchel cookies
in foil for my mother
who liked them with tea.

Outside, on the busy street,
we fed the food to the car trunk's
open mouth. I was back
in Worcester, Massachusetts.
It was November 1978 and
the city buses and eight-cylinder cars
anxiously gulped after rumors of rationing.

ONE IN A MILLION

Ballad-hungry men gathered around the young deck hand.
Tired of shanties, they closed their eyes to make believe
the boy's falsetto was that of a woman.
Each face revealed a bit about his envisioned lady.
Even the singer's eye shut to help him
best feel his chest flutter to the swaying beat.

A gull hovered.
The oldest salt sighed through his mouth.
Chafing wood planks squeaked.
Under his long coat, the widower captain
pinched his thigh to refrain from weeping.

Kindly, time waited for the song's end, but not much longer.
The treacherous reef bit into the ship, as if starving.
As if it would never again come across such a meal.
The hull filled quickly.
On-deck men felt the sun soak into their skin
as their shoes filled with the sea.

In Nazaré, a wife sings that same doomed ballad
as she hangs cod on racks set in the sand.
Old women listen to the fish-drying wind
harmonize with her melody.
They remember wanting.
They remember waiting.
She sings alone.
Passing time, lingering until a homecoming,
while his ship rests on the ocean floor.

FROM FEMALE TO MALE

Robust hugs, handshakes that remember
Comrade, you
turn inside out
to hush the monthly glitch.

Who could contain the boy inside,
sweet-faced countless exits ago?
Pupils are question marks
in the spotlight and in the bathroom.

Are we ourselves?
Are we heroes?
Are we soldiers?
Are we mistaken for > men < ?

Soft-hearted, hard-headed ally,
Where's the time gone?
Somewhat cheating,
we were busy being boys.

You interrogate
your chest, heavy with craving
for boundless free-range flatlands.

Your temple's interior
The hidden side of your skin
The four quarters of your heart
Do they breathe relief
when you shoot Mr. T?

TERESA
DE LA CRUZ

One Particular Woman

TERESA DE LA CRUZ was born
and raised in San Jose, California.
She earned a Bachelor's of Arts
in Creative Writing from San
Francisco State University. She
loves hockey, tortillas, and wine.

G7 TO G5

i recall you surreal and raw.
uncooked conceit with two dirty paws,
so adept beneath the moonbeams
in nothing but a bra.

so we kissed and other things.
dropped gun slings and stings,
but the fervor still
rendered my prints on your wings.

IMPULSE

I want to have sex
in the dark corner
around the bend, vacillate
between the riffs
of one another...quietly
because there is a lecture
on the other side of the door
and our vibe
is enough to permeate
the cracks of academia.

G

lightning strikes
lashes ebb
rivulets dry
upon sheets

walls collapse
fingers dance
overtures cease
under fire

her remnants
wide angle
abdomen smooth
digging deep

O

ocean hues
silver swagger
carom through
veins

so electric
the regard
to erupt
and transfix

sweet nothings
olive skin
brewing for
bone

LOVING A GRAVE

I ran in the trigger
to pull the rain

I drove our favorite song
listening to a stolen car

I was wiping vodka
and drinking tears...

because loving a grave
is digging you.

VODKA, VODKA, GUN

we argued.
she left.
shot glass.

we stopped talking.
i left.
shot glass.

i cried.
you did not.
trigger.

MUTUALITY

my mind and my mother are
separated

maybe i am mutant alien blood
and molecules misbehave

maximizing the morsels
making muscles ache

my mind and my mother are
mute

maybe I am merely
misunderstood

missing my mother

motherfucker

MOTHER

Mother Earth
Mother love

Mother ship
Mother sing

Mother womb
Mother wound

Mother fucker
Mother phantom

Mother please
Mother cease

Mother maybe
       appease

ECHOES THAT ROAM

The grass and silhouette
with strings that circumvent

The rock and instruments
like love and incidents

The poppy is happenstance
the song has aftermath

The roots and energy
like stardust and purity

The seeds and bone
are echoes that roam

LITTLE CAT FEET

The fog comes
on little cat feet.
— *C. Sandburg*

It is not yet 4am and your little cat feet
stroll across my sleep

You sense the phantoms and lick me awake
with a granular tongue

As I catch my breath you lay on my hip
poised with a sentinel stare.

THE ID

we were in the room

      topless.   just having sex   and

      eating oreos.

BODY PARTS

1.   There is a permanent left thumbprint
     on the soft protruding edge of her pelvic bone

     that is where I grab her when rhythm
     begins to emulate the brumal waves of the North Shore.

2.   Her naked backside was the downbeat,
     my middle finger sliding down her spine...

     the arpeggio

3.   She sleeps so lovely
     under the dusk appellation light
     as the vines unfurl
     from the breeze off her nape

A DOZEN IMAGES

snake blood in a shot glass.

iodine through a syringe.

placenta of a stillborn.

a mosquito digging in.

layers of cooled lava.

a five dollar shake.

the messy tip of a quill.

a cluster of roe on a plate.

shark saliva breaking skin.

absinthe and a sugar cube.

fight club bar of soap.

the pearly harbor residue.

BECAUSE OF A FEW POEMS

Because of a few poems
women have taken their clothes off
for me.

They like to rub
my words
all over their naked bodies.
It makes them smile
in their own different ways.

I've seen them all,
pretty girls I mean.
Some in Superlover costumes,
some with their clever tricks.

This one girl
entered my pinky with her pinky,
she cruised my palm through inward knees,
with her clammy skin and dirty nail
the end of summer had begun.

Another girl
wanted some love in a darkroom.
She was a slapshot.
And my shirt still has the fixer stains.

I saw one woman
shimmy shake out of her dress
after one of my haikus.
She was also seventeen syllables.
And her purple walls collapsed
in seconds.

Because of a few poems
some women became slow bullets
needing to test the waters
of organic senses
and pace around
their flickering curiosities.

One particular woman
was kind enough to share

a mental backfire with me.
She was the worst papercut between all my webs.
She was a particular flicker
this particular way   about her...
and I'm still not sure
what really happened.

But the current woman,
this last woman
is a slow chemical reaction.
She has writing for days,
keeps me searching for pens.
She loves my words,
the things they say.
My words love her,
with her lashes like line breaks,
her mouth like an inkwell.
She is still
piece by piece
all the beautiful words

unfolding.

MY GLOSSARY OF TERMS

once (adverb)

1.   I kissed a girl once, and I haven't stopped kissing her since.

2.   Once is a moment for everyone; see also *moment*

pastry (noun)

1.   Her pheromone is the perfect combination of sugar and zest; she is an extract I want to imbibe.

ribcage (noun)

1.   Some women vomit to see their own ribcage. The things those women read show pictures of "pretty women" arching their backs, extending their breasts...opening themselves to all hands and knives, opening themselves to their twisted truths and shattered hives.

2.   Evolution put all my important organs under the ribcage, thus I put all my important things there too (*i.e. you*).

vintage (adjective)

1.   your vintage fedora on the floor = a bullet my memory can't shake

instructions (noun)

1.   I did not purposely throw away the instructions for loving a man, but I did not purposely keep them either.

JULIE R. ENSZER

DE FIDELIS

JULIE R. ENSZER is author of *Handmade Love* (A Midsummer Night's Press, 2010) and *Sisterhood* (Seven Kitchens Press, 2010). In 2011, she edited *Milk and Honey: A Celebration of Jewish Lesbian Poetry* (A Midsummer Night's Press). She earned an MFA from the University of Maryland and is currently enrolled in its PhD program in Women's Studies.

BEGINNINGS

In Michigan, September dusk is chilly.
We linger in the parking garage
of the downtown Millender Center.
Wind whips through concrete;
the sun sets. Cars cruise by, we identify
makes and models from internal
combustion, the squeal of turning tires,
running engines. Our ears, expert
at this exercise. Neither wants to leave
the other. Polite conversation exhausted,
we turn to taboo. What we dream,
secret hopes, aspirations. We've touched
only once (when you brushed my hand
to light a cigarette), when I tell you,
you must stop coming in my dreams.
Twenty-four hours later, each leaving
other lovers, we begin life together.

SWEATER

I am wearing a cream, cable sweater,
cotton with a cowell. It is my favorite.
First worn from the wash; line dry
required; often, too eager, I wear
it damp. Still shapen and knit tight,
it is formal for meetings,
comfortable for gathering with friends.
Two years later, this sweater is a sweet
reminiscence of our fall together,
until you spill oily food—salad dressing,
perhaps, a creamy alfredo. The sweater,
destroyed. No wash can clean it.
I never find a proper replacement.

BED

The first year even the best-made
beds in cold climes lie naked.
Sheets and covers cast aside.
Oil companies make profits
on the backs of new lovers.
Once we would wake at five,
talk through sunrise, then rush to work.
Home again, we resume
what we regard as our real lives.
Later, early sojourns turn from intimate
discoveries to shared anxieties.
Phone calls pierce darkness
with bad news, and pillows,
matted or lumpy, absorb
more tears that muffled screams.
For a while, our angry cat, Gertie, pees
on the bed despite constant litter
cleaning and multiple vet trips.
Sometimes, between three and four a.m.
on a break from her game
of bridge, your dead mother visits,
I tell her about our life as if it matters.
She strokes your hair and smiles.

CLOSET

In the hallway
wearing only socks
just as I drop my head
to your shoulder
and you press your fingers
toward contractions,
someone knocks.
The dogs scuffle
then break into canine song.

So soon after the breakup,
you whisper, *Oh, no,*
It might be her.
Here—in the closet—
you hide me naked.

The floor is piled with shoes,
bent hangers,
thin dry-cleaning bags.
In darkness, I root
for a robe.
Then, laughter.

Meekly, you open
the door. *This—*
is my friend—
I stick out my hand,
then draw it away.
Musty, glistening.
Evidence of what
was interrupted.

DISHES

On our first Saturday together,
I tackle your kitchen.
Plates, pots, and pans piled
in the sick, on the counters,
in the stove. Too old to be rotten.
Just crusty, petrified. You advise,
just throw out that pan;
I'll buy another. But soap, hot water, and
scrubbing clean and shine them all.
Now I want to whisper to
my younger self: Passion fades.
You will always be doing the dishes.

DISTRESS

This is never captured by Hollywood:
anxiety after each of you leave
another to be together.
We spend years worried
about each new friend or
acquaintance. New evening activities—
political campaigning,
card clubs, poetry readings—
any late night out, leaves one
at home to wonder,
will the day come
when we rehash the well-trod line,
this is the best day of my life,
as it becomes the worst of mine?

HEREDITY

My anxiety, compounded
by family history—
her father's first child born
six months and one year
after he married her mother
(this was ten years before
she was adopted) and
a quarter century before she,
at fourteen, picked up
the telephone to overhear
her father's amorous imbroglio.
Two years later, her parents divorce.
She declares to me her fealty
but I worry, what if infidelity
is passed in families?

RINGS

Near Valentine's Day,
we buy rings on a lark,
though we do not save them as gifts,
just get them sized.
Mine, a permanent resident on my right finger;
Hers, an occasional embellishment.
When asked about marriage,
I hold out my left hand, bare.
We say, we'll marry
when it's legal in our state.
This makes me feel perfectly safe
until I hear of European tradition
that adorns the right hand
with the wedding ring.
I think of all the continentals
considering me married.
Customs are never easy.
Still, with no band—
no initials and date inscribed—
we date our existence like scientists
testing for radiation emissions,
marking half-lives.

APOGEE

The hardest year was seven,
not an itch but an irritation
that persisted.
I resented the repeated
need to shop,
run a household,
mostly the way she enjoys these things.
I wanted time for myself.
Now I see people at this point
in their marriage, they ask,
how did it pass? The truth
makes me look bad.
My lover's mother
was sick and suddenly her death
was in sight and I, not wanting
to be the sort of woman who leaves,
tried to stop complaining,
(she will tell you I didn't but I tried);
I cleaned, made arrangements
for a dozen trips.
Hotel and rental car
reservations. Packed
luggage with small gifts,
even assembled Easter
baskets for mother and daughter.
We knew how the story would end.
Then I couldn't be the woman
who left another grieving.
By the time
the veil of loss lifted,
we were honeymooning again.

COINCIDENTAL

When my sister reads
my father's email one
Christmas Eve, she calls me
the next day, angry.
Her voice, drawn, thin, dark.
She demands, *Did you know?*
Did you know? As though
we were in some secret fraternity
with every member carefully
vetted, reviewed, and approved.
She doesn't understand
how capacious the questions of sex.
How it seems almost accidental—
you share a cabin at summer camp,
you meet a woman about whom you've dreamed.
I imagine it this way for my father,
meeting someone willing in his sixties.
I hope for the same virility,
but my sister is just seething in anger,
my mother in shock and disbelief,
and I must admit
I never expected infidelity
to visit my family.

SEVENTY

Growing up too young to be
a child of the sixties, I am aware
that sex in the seventies was different,
somehow special, exciting
and, aided by powerful antibiotics,
without fear or precautions.
While my homosex was tempered
by the specter of premature death,
some recall sex without inhibitions.
In this tradition, I think of sex in the seventies
with longing, even yearning,
until it becomes not sex in the seventies
but sex in one's seventies,
a concept I'm forced to consider
when my beloved's uncle
tells us he's been unfaithful to his wife
of thirty-some years.
More than relatives, they were correlative:
marriage and happiness
retirement and joy
lover and companion.
Now my aunt, reduced to mistrust and misgivings,
confides, "He's addicted to the oral sex."
This makes me worry,
someday the same accusation will be flung at me,
but for now only he's called
to account for these transgressions.

JUDGMENT

I quip to friends—
it's inspiring to see untamed desire
propagate among the retired.
we'd like to imagine ourselves
horny at sixty-seven,
getting it on with a new one at sixty-eight,
committing cunnilingus at sixty-nine,
all just foreplay to wild sex in the seventies.
Gales of laughter erupt and spill all around,
but it's not true.
We're moralistic in our thirties and forties,
as shocked by their new adolescence
as they once purported to be by ours.

DEMUR

Now I wonder about our uncle's visits
to Thailand—R&R from the military.
I think of the person who gave me
a foot massage the week I was there.
He—or she—I couldn't tell—rubbed
my toes, my heels, my calves,
proceeded up my thighs
until I opened my eyes.
Thank you, I said. Then she—or he—
(I confess, I like to know the gender,
it is central to my sense of orientation)
stopped. Did he, like me,
not simply say, *Thank you?*

CONJUGAL

When did we first demand exclusivity?
Who deemed it so?
Surely not G-d, the primordial polyamor.
She loves us all.
Adam had the inaugural "starter" marriage,
leaving Lilith to enjoy her later days as a singleton.
The Torah tells the truth—
lust and love break down to betrayal—
G-d mocks us: you've been forewarned.
As though forewarned is forearmed.
As though there are armaments
to wage this war beyond our flesh,
beyond our feeble hearts and
wayward minds,
beyond our hungry tongues.

DEVOTED

For years I wanted to be my aunt,
direct, plain-spoken,
clear about priorities.
Beginning with family but extending to a wide array
of social and ethical responsibilities.
And you, my beloved, I fancied you, your uncle,
enjoying the flurry of activities,
and even the occasional nattering.
One year, they took six cruises.
Visited every port on the planet,
but travel didn't bring them closer.
We fear it may never be enough:
miles, apologies, moral accounting.
We watch the unraveling of family,
knowing now we can be neither—he nor she.
We hold to one another,
though never too tightly.

PERFUME

Thirteen years since
my wife left you for me,
I think about the perfume
she bought you for birthdays
and anniversaries. My own
temples bare of sweet
scents from the beautiful bottles
you lined atop your dresser.
I wonder about their fate.
Was there one day
when you sprayed
the last drop? Or on this day,
now our anniversary,
did you, in anger,
throw them all out?

STOLEN

Sometimes, rinsing the dishes
as I load the washer,
sponging small pieces of lettuce,
clumps of parmesan cheese
in creamy Caesar dressing,
I think this isn't my life.
It is the life I stole from you.
I've made it mine—
installed a tile floor with grout
that needs to be cleaned,
purchased sturdy, daily dishes,
bought food with your money.
Cleaning the refrigerator,
moving jars and cans and bottles
bits of produce from the farm,
I take out the shelves,
wash them in warm soapy water,
replace the box of baking soda.
I want this life to be clean,
free from odors,
if you come back.
If you return to claim it.

RECONCILE

Everything that has brought me
to this moment in my life
every movie I've seen
every book I've read
every philosophy I've espoused
every ideology I've studied
tells me I should hate
this uncle, my father,
my beloved's father...
but I can't. All old men.
Ineffably human.
I am they.
Each day, I walk out the door.
It is a choice.
How I return.

CODA

Once I believed marriage was received,
separate from the self,
a third thing to which two people cleave.
Concrete—a large antique chest
not finely made, but utilitarian,
the kind that moves from farmhouse
to garage to first apartment.
Or long-lasting sheets, part polyester,
given to family members in need.
Marriage isn't like that.
As much as it's shared,
it's an individual burden
or gift—depends on the day—
like this morning,
I meet a gorgeous woman
wearing old Levis, a silk shirt,
and suddenly I am my uncle,
sleeping with his brother's wife.
I am my father with a clandestine lover.
Indiscretion is easy.
There is nothing to stop me.
Today, I make a different choice.

GINA R. EVERS

THE MAPS INSIDE

GINA R. EVERS's work has appeared in *Copper Nickel*, *shady side review*, and the anthology *One for the Road*, and poems here have been featured in *Bloom* and *In Capital Letters*. She has been honored with a first prize and an honorable mention in *IC View*'s 2010 annual literary and arts contest. Also in 2010, the Lambda Literary Foundation named her as an Emerging LGBT Voice. Originally from Chicago, Gina now lives and works in Washington, DC.

AIR RAID
For Nonna

There were no windows
                anymore.
No ceiling or roof
             to shield us from the sky.

Mother couldn't cook,
               afraid the cracks
of hot oil
         would mask the siren.

When it called, the air
              became thick
and we all were pushed
                into the small shelter.

We were quiet
          like meat in its grinder.
The soldiers' horses
           closest to the door

choking back their winnies
                until it stopped.
As we marched back
          the earth

from the dirt floor
            powdered the air
like the smoke and ash
             from dried sage

my mother burned
           to bless each morning.

BOUNDARIES

Behind sawdust-veiled air, screeching and pounding,
my grandfather built furniture. He couldn't speak English,
couldn't talk about the war. In twelve-hour shifts, he hid pieces of himself
in the copper knobs, in the waves of carved woodwork like the coast of the Adriatic—
a home he had lost and, then, shut away inside an attic trunk.
Now the trunk's in my mother's basement, still concealing the framed map:
the Istrian peninsula inside Italian borders. After his funeral, Mamma sat
fingering the leg of an endtable. She said they didn't tell the soldiers what was going on
in the war camps. He was only fighting to keep the farmhouse he was born in,
for his brothers and his new wife who he wanted to take there
to live always bumped up with the sea. I used to watch his fingertips,
yellowed with tobacco, tearing through skin and yanking bones from mackerels.
The fish's steamed eyes shone like sequins as he ripped pieces of flesh
and placed them onto my tongue: salty and dry; his fingers bitter.

MAMMA'S 500 LIRE COIN

Silver-rimmed gold,
talisman in her pocket:
Counter curse for *malocchio*—the eye—
sockets in Carnevale masks,
round baskets stacked with fresh fish,
their lips like full moons.
My grandparents' round cheeks,
fat with mollusks, at the center
of that spiraling marketplace.

Curved hulls tethered to the Adriatic—
A barge's rails ringed with bodies,
barrels of bread, life preserver.
Nonna's hands cupping a rosary.
Anxious faces behind portholes.
A gold window with a silver sill.

MIA FARFALLA
—MY BUTTERFLY—
To Mary

My nonna is the only woman
who ever called me something other

than my own name. When I was a girl
her words nuzzled the bridge of my nose

all of their feet padding
soft wells beneath my eyes.

When she said it, I could see each scale—
sapphire and the moon-blue alabaster

that only exists in Venetian mosaics—
a wingspan of azure lenses

too big for my face.
Now a woman, I am not the type

to tattoo a butterfly on my back.
But when you grasp my hand—having never

discussed it—and point to Eastern Tiger Swallowtail
to Mourning Cloak sunning itself

on the red-brick-painted-white of this city.
When you cradle that fistful of seeds

before planting Zinnia and Cosmos in the biology
of our backyard, clacking

the dirt off your trowel, digging
ungloved fingers down and deep

your browbone stained darker
after every smear, and finally

look up at me from under the brim
of your ridiculous gardening hat

I forget—for a moment—
to care what people call me.

TO SHAME

After Jane Kenyon

1. *In My Blood*

My family brought you.
Boarded with you in Venice
using words with rolling Rs, sirens
blaring *wrong side of the war*
each time they parted their lips.

Thirty years gone
and you grew bored
with their tattered trunk—purged
of the markers of their difference.
I was born and you crept
from its corners,
cozied up in my bronchioles,
decided to wait.

Sara and I had finished
touching in the girls bathroom.
At the edge of the schoolyard
I saw my friend with the pretty hair
curling around his olive face.

There was a boy twisting his arms
holding him between the young tree
and the thick wire staked into the ground
to make the tree grow straight,
ensure it would be tall as the sky.

There was another boy, too,
who pulled back the cable,
aimed it. And they chanted
with the music of the wire:
Faggot! Faggot!

I thought: He is my friend!
He is in fifth grade
and sits with me at Kaptain Kid.
My friend! Who drinks orange juice
inside the playhouse
where we pretend it's tea.

I didn't understand
how he and I were alike, but I ran
like you told me to.
I ran fast, past a police car.
And now, I can't say for sure
the police car was really there.
Or if it is only you
planting a bomb into my memory.

2. *A Secret*

I think the word: lesbian
sounds like a skin disease
(even after ten years
saying that is what I am).
Erythrasma. Tinea
Unguium. Lesbian.

Each time someone says it at me
a glass of ice water in my face.
Every time
someone makes me wear it.

3. *Role Models*

Every Wednesday we ran the mile
and lined up in the locker room
for the showers.

Mrs. Flagg stood at the other end of the wall
to catch our towels
before we paraded naked
through rows of spitting shower heads.
She watched, marking her clipboard,
terrycloth hostage in her fist.

Soon as Mrs. Flagg left the locker room
Kary would yell,
You can't get away with this.
I'm going to have my father arrest you!
But she never did.

Instead she kicked in the stall
where Erin was dressing.

Erin, with her blazing, curly mullet,
her button-up shirt, her black jeans, gym shoes.

Hiding your dick in this stall, Erin?
Gonna come in for private showers with The Fagg after school?
I know you like how she watches.

4. *Once*

Once, toward the end of the seven years
between when I knew and when I said it
out loud, I opened the Bible.

Mamma taught me to pray,
showed me how to offer lilies
to St. Anthony. Holding my hand, she walked
the stations of the cross, kissed only
my left palm, where I received the host
because it was pure and led to my heart.

So when I begged Jesus,
for seven years, to make me normal
and He answered,

"Daughter, go in peace, for your faith
has healed you."

I thought I had been cured.

How is it possible that you
are more powerful than God?

5. *Boyfriend*

I hovered over the bowl,
mascara streaming into the water,
esophagus burning as I choked,
I want... to date girls.

I know, he said,
and reached over my head
for the toilet paper.

6. *Mother Tongue*

I was sure you were gone
when I sat at the table
and told Mamma.
You returned
quietly slithering

constricting around me,
hissing incantations as I spoke.
It was your voice that emerged
from her lips:
non é normale—
and don't expect me
to be proud.

In Italian, I do not know
the word for lesbian.
I only know: *Fica! Fica!*

7. *Comment from a Stranger*

Isn't your daughter a little old
to be holding your hand?

8. *Weddings*

There is no Chuppah. No Mehndi, Kikombe,
or Rings. No Gathbandhan, Broomjumps, Handfasting.
No Blendings, no Rice, no Seven Blessings.
At Brandon's ceremony police sirens
made the sanctuary hold its breath.
They passed over and he joked: *They know*
what's going on in here. Everyone laughed.
It was easier than being afraid.

9. *Running*

On Sundays I suck the air,
the smell of woods
hiding sewer lines
behind my apartment,
in through the nose and out
through the mouth
like Mrs. Flagg taught me.

When my lungs begin to strain
I look to the ground, to the leaves
and tell myself they are hiding
sharp rocks, roots that will trip me.

But I make it to the fallen log
same as always.
It's a different kind of endurance,
attempting to be better.

A NATION OF IMMIGRANTS

Hair toweled wild, my lover
comes back to bed—Dove soap
ignoring our ginger, cinnamon.
Pressing my hips down,
I ballast her brass bedframe,
rocking like the old Venetian boat
that delivered my mother.

Italians have been coming
since the beginning, since Cristoforo
put on his Spanish mask.
Changing faces for gold, for opportunity,
we're good at tossing names aside;
good at living flat in the boundaries of Illinois
but calling it India.

Inside her body, we sail
and I'm conscious of Mamma's figure
fading into the shadows
cast by rising sun—
dark as the farmhouse,
as her nonna's face
the morning she left.

She leaves—late for work—
I float in the folds of aqua,
whetted by the new world
beyond the coastline
of Ms. Liberty's robe and slip.

TERRA FIRMA

You named me butterfly—
                creature incapable

of nest-building,
          a haunted migrant,

constantly seeking
               citrus and warmer winds.

Forgetting your omen,
          you call me Gypsy—*Zingara*—

               forgetting it was you who taught me
to open the world's fists,

read the maps inside
          pushing leave! *vai!*

I understand
      you crossed the Atlantic

when the war drew life lines:
             your Pola excised from Italy,

leaving your mother behind.
                You don't understand

how I could follow
        blue lines

in another woman's body—
           heart lines, fate lines

growing like wings,
         rivers on an unfolding map.

Please, call me granddaughter.
           Call me earthworm.

Call me immigrant—
      you make it look easy

as Easter afternoon sun
              pressed against venetian blinds.

Outside, children
         chalk circles on sidewalk,

marking boundaries, laughing:
             Stay away!

That land is yours,
         and this land is mine.

CAYUGA LAKESHORE. $250K. 1.5 BATHS.

For Mary

At 2 a.m. I'm not worried about the money
only about you sleeping well after our fight—
this city and the cat and my cubicle and time.
The alarm will go off at five, you will tell me
to move to the bed. Remember
that drive up Route 89, honeysuckle wind,
the lake billowing to our right—in and out
through the hills—and how when we stopped
to pick wild strawberries you pulled
fistfuls of garlic mustard
so it wouldn't strangle the young flowers?
Yesterday I walked to the subway
and saw a girl, maybe she was four,
raising a carrot in her tiny fist.
Its green tendons a starving sea anemone
reaching through the exhaust, through filmy steam
wafting from the sidewalk grate she stood on.
Beaming, the girl showed everyone who would look
what it is to have a little, orange piece of earth to hold onto.

POMEGRANATE

As Mary bloodies the countertop,
I think of Persephone's mother
who made winter—six seeds.
Six months in the hospital
when I was princess of the black chamber too.
Mamma's ear pressed to the plateau of my back
listening to the wheeze,
pleading my pulmonary self to re-awaken,
to climb out of the diaphragmed dark
kicking muscles between each rung of my ribcage
so they might be spurred into contraction,
that slow drawing in and release I re-learned
to breathe spring. Mary uses her fingers
to scoop swollen arils, hollowing a cavity in the lobes.
She presses her cheek to my breast, says *you're wheezing.*
But my lungs are only making the noise of translation,
sputtering through languages so both understand:
the pneuma in my chest has grown into a river.
It has filled pools in the courtyards of both worlds
and waits now at the ferry, even as they eavesdrop,
faces pressed to my back and front banks.

REFUGEE

My mother had been watching
the poultryman wrestle his sack
as Yugoslavian border patrol
quartered the cars of her train.
Feathers exploding, he bit the bottlecap
spilling grappa down their gizzards
before kicking canvas under his seat,
sedating, muffling the birds' *schiamazzi*.
Maybe it was longing to see her nonna's farm,
the home they were forced to flee
after the war, the Paris Peace Treaty,
when they could no longer be Italian.
Or maybe it was her new, American innocence—
the immigrant girl goes home an alien,
not yet having learned to fear authority—
that shot her arm into the air
when the officer asked
about *animali illegali, droghe.*

It's a slow slaughter,
being liquored into silence.
A femme in a dyke bar, I am listening
to how nobody is cis-gendered anymore,
as though my name for the ocean
doesn't make it wet.

I wish I could speak queerness
like I can speak Italian.

Even in full immersion, the linguistics
of lipstick gender performance,
gold star, vanilla,
right-pocket flagging
makes queer liberation
name me: hetero-
normative assimilationist.
I am tired
of feeling like a foreigner.

If only someone knew where I came from
he could lift his melting pot mask
and tell me to go back there.

There, a place of food for desire
where rocks jut over waves
and we are taught how to climb them.
Where home can be more than a repressed memory:
a recipe for *risi e bisi* flooding my conscience
as I stick to the bar, her knee wedged
between my legs, her hand scalding my thigh—
Nonna's wooden spoon scraping
a clean line along the bottom of the pan and—
oh God—sautéing mushrooms hot
and slick, falling through my fingers.
She pushes my hand away.

My mother's wrist was yanked
by Soviet border patrol.
It popped her shoulder out of its socket
just as we're all popped out of ourselves
soon as we start questioning.
Is *huhn, gallina, kokoška,* or *chicken*
the word that fits in our mouths?
What is the name for the thing
we think we're saving?
And before we can begin to articulate our bodies
or name hunger for wholeness longing,
before we even spit a consonant, customs
shove us back into our compartments.

Shut up while he makes an example
of the man who plucks at the borders.
Shut up so we can keep safe, keep traveling.

ANDY IZENSON

CARRIED BY THESE THINGS

ANDY IZENSON is a genderfluid queer law student, activist, and event planner living in New York City. She has been writing poetry since she figured out how to hold a pencil, and this is her first publication. You can see her poetry blog at

ForTheSameReasonIBreathe.tumblr.com

T-SHIRT

Dearest butches,
I am not always a girl,
but when I am, it is for you.
Your oversized t-shirts make me feel
small, protectable,
wrapped in an exoskeleton of your strength.
I know your boots are heavy
and that you know my stilettos hurt
and that I wear them for your eyes on me.
And when I can wake up surrounded by you
by your warm, rough hands and tattoo-spangled skin, then—
girl, boi, femme, twink, pup, woman—
I'm yours.

HUMORS

There are words inside my cunt.
Feel for them with your tongue. They are hot words,
multisyllabic murmurs and flutters of words,
glinting wet strung-together letters that will stretch and sway
between us when you lift your mouth away. My cunt oozes these words
generously, offers them up to you like a supplicant,
take them. Read them, hear them, feel my cunt,
feel it like fertile earth, words springing out,
rich with whispers and cries and dancing fingers across Braille lips.
I can write my cunt. I can wrap my hand around a pen
and I can let the words flow up from my loquacious wetness
and slick slip out in the ink in a silky circuit. I can wipe opulent words
from my sticky fingers onto a willing page. I can write my cunt.
I cannot write my heart. My heart
is an arid, derivative organ, dry clenching muscle,
fields watered with salt and baked under the sun
of a day whose dawn has been stolen
by too many lovers' eyes, whose twilight
has been drained by too many poets
with over-eager romantic sensibilities.
There is no sunset left here, and no moisture.
Parched words, stuttering, a melancholic humor like pens all run dry,
clammy yellow bile. No words. No rhythm.
It can produce no original shred
and will give you nothing.
Leave it. Come instead
to the home of my words, to the home of my hunger,
my wild song, to where the beauty pours out of me
and leaves gossamer shards on your clothing and lower lip.
Dip yourself into the unfolding sanguinity of it; leave my heart.
For you, I write my cunt.

CHROMOSYLUM

I am a haven for all the unwanted pieces of genders. I am
held together with steel hooks
and steel eyes,
a crude seam running from throat to hip,
from scalp to scapula, across my cheekbone and down my left leg.

I have learned to speak carefully
and I have been taught to walk in heels.
I have practiced shaving and swaggering
and slinking and squatting and simpering
and drinking beer and putting on eyeliner
and spitting on the sidewalk
and I have come to understand the constellation
of meaning carried by these things.

What would I be had I not taken these lessons?
What would I be built of if every transgression had not resulted
in a ruler-crack across my knuckles, knuckles-crack across my jaw?

I carefully apply lipstick to my front teeth. I
rip apart, seams tearing with a
sound like old
metal. I
whimper when injured like an animal.
I am failing to be free—

I am failing,
to be free.

PAPERWEIGHT

For once I get to be the tide, the seducer,
letting you let me in,
opening instead of being opened,
guiding my pen across you as
I please,
I push, I write your cries
and the brightness on your lower lip, your eyes,
in the heartbeats before they happen
and in slick ink across your belly.

The subjective case feels heavy and powerful,
I fuck, I fuck, I *fuck,* I savor
the structure and carry myself, us,
deeper and deeper again.

This time I get to lay my weight on you
as you shake,
I am the one who is the ballast for your erasure,
who keeps the heat inside you,
keeps it from sinking your skin
into my sheets,
and we are both the ones leaking words
in declensions unknown,
wetly across our bodies.

TOXAPHENE

You belong in the green and gold of perpetual summer,
where that shape I thought I'd never see outside of your smile
becomes apparent in every drop of warm honey rain that falls into still water.
Change out the silver in your lip for blades of grass,
weave pine needles into the lines that will form
at the corners of your eyes,
and let dew pool behind your collarbones from sitting still, so still.
Even the frogs won't protest when you kneel, defiant, in the twilight,
because they, and this place, are your audience and do not exist outside
of this mown-grass-smelling dusk. And finally,
when the night is swollen with August,
you can find the tiny path of chill in the air,
you can follow it through the labyrinthine dark,
laying out the trail ahead of your feet.
Even as you walk you'll reel it in behind you,
you'll wind it up around your heart like a coiled snake,
and nobody will follow you to autumn.

CYTHERA

I saw a goddess on the subway this morning,
a bleach-blonde aphrodite rising on the swell of the Inbound Red Line,
serene, electric,
the delicate smear of her lips curved like her son's mesmerizing bow.
A swagger in her stance as she wrapped one hand—
(nails short, bitten, chipped black)
—around the scepter of the subway pole and swayed
with the motions of the car like the reeds
that moan over Syrinx's tomb.

What taste, I wondered, infused that ivory jaw?
Cologne? Smoke? Coffee and old cloves?

I watched her climb the platform
stairs to some Olympian destination
off of Park Street
and knew—

Her skin would taste of incense, of olives.
Of fever dreams.

BITTERS

I am bluer than curaçao
and a dozen times more twisted up
than the corkscrew curls on your wig.
Dress yourself in bourbon and gold
to match the Jose lines painting
themselves down from the corners of your mouth.
Dame means such nothing, such
transience in your angostura voice,
like I could give you anything but really,
how long would it be before the glass slipped
from your nerveless olive fingers,
shimmered to the filthy tile?
No longer, I might tell the tap's hiss,
than it would take me to drink you,
to sip at your heat damp skin
with cosmopolitan lips until your eyes
are bone-empty, until only melting
rocks remain and I find myself
cradling dead soldier,
or straight up,
twist of regret.

STORM

Your kiss is the wind, beautiful girl.
Don't tell me you have to go.

I'll stand on my toes
on your toes
just to reach the rice paper of your eyelids

just to lay my fingers across your throat.

Your hands are tide-licked bone
and I must confess

I'm a little afraid
of how easily we could
blow away.

Or how easily we could snap,
tangled as we are into that space between two heartbeats—
my fists locked around your bird bones
and your teeth clenched
on my ear.

I wouldn't mean to do it, but
you see, I've just discovered
this vein of cruelty running through me.

I always mean to touch you tenderly,

I always try! But your skin, somehow,
begs for bruises

and the hurricane of your sobbing
is such an enchanting sound.

Tell me, please, that when I drink away your rain,
your smile will come out,

you'll assure me that I read
you right,

let me kiss your typhoon eyes.

STRAWBERRY

I had a poetry professor once tell me
that every poem is a love poem.
Well, this one is not.
This is a lust poem.
This is a knees on a hardwood floor poem,
a smack of your leather belt poem,
a fingers in my mouth poem,
a grip on my hair until my neck, waist, knees, collapse poem,
and a fist-sized bruise on the back of my right thigh for a week and a half poem.
It's a sweat jewelling your nose poem
and a poem for my knees over your shoulders and my teeth tearing your comforter.
I don't fall in love
and I don't write love poems.
So this is a tangling of fingers and biting away of moans poem,
a kissing strawberries from your mouth
in a dark stairwell poem,
an eyelashes against my cheek poem,
a poem for you holding me down and holding me down and holding me,
and a poem for your dimples when I call you mine.

RONNA MAGY

MEMORY FROM BONE

RONNA MAGY is a lesbian senior who came onto the planet as the colors of World War II were fading from Detroit's skyline and Sputnik orbited the skies. She began writing at mid-life. Her stories and poetry have appeared in journals and anthologies including: *Sinister Wisdom*; *Best Lesbian Romance*; *My Life is Poetry*; *Hers 2*; *Love Shook My Heart II*; *Heatwave*; and *The Bilingual Review*. She is the author of several English as a Second Language textbooks.

THE AVENUE OF FASHION

Along Livernois near Seven Mile, the Avenue of Fashion around the corner from our Detroit house growing up, women richer than my family shop for dresses and hats, shoes and scarves, and silk stockings. Get their hair done at Franklin Beauty Salon and have their finger nails painted post-war, Canary-red, to match their lipstick. Beautiful women, rich women, the kind who spend afternoons playing bridge, and don't have to work.

Those women whose daughters I go to Pasteur Elementary School with, whose everyday maids take Thursdays off. And on that day, and every Thursday, the daughters go to Town House Restaurant for lunch.

I beg my mother to let me go with them, be like those girls who live in the two-story brick houses on the other side of Livernois, get their hair done weekly, eat greasy hamburgers and French fries, play Love and Marriage on the juke box, and talk four at a table, on Thursdays, at noon at the Town House Restaurant, before returning to Mr. Matthews' 6th grade class.

Those girls, Marilyn, Candy, and Diane, have money, are beautiful, wear pretty new clothes, and go around together at school. I want to be just like them. Wear the skirts and matching sweaters they wear, eat what they eat, live in their brick houses; I want to be one of them.

But we're not like them, my mother tells me. You shouldn't compare yourself to them. We're different, she says. Different than those girls who live on the other side of Livernois, the other side of the Avenue of Fashion.

ROUND PIE

so circumscribed, so round, those childhood days,
like the pie tins grandma pulled from the oven,
green apple slices bubbling over oven-browned crusts,
layers of sugar piled on top.
wedges of days layered with polite dresses,
saddle shoes and ivory soap,
post world war.
round seven-day weeks
that folded one day into another,
circled and contained
the family world
in which I was
brought up.

so hard they tried to
separate our lives from
the war, concentration camps, and industrial waste,
those manufactured Detroit days
during which I was raised.
Chryslers showcased
in glass showrooms 'round town
while factories lined the city's core.
Fords and Dodges steering their way along Woodward,
as Sputnik roamed the skies.

downtown, near the Detroit River,
newspaper strewn chain-link fences
held in the poor,
while in red brick houses on the northwest side,
behind double-paned windows,
we stood safe from the cold.

BLACK SILK

Black silk smoothed between fingers reminds me of her skin, the way I'd run my hands from her shoulders down along her breasts to her nipples until they were hard, down along her belly, down to her clit. The way she'd undulate and move like a palm tree swaying in a tropical breeze when we made love against the wall. How her sounds of "oh" and "touch me here" rose above the whirring ceiling fan. The way we'd come onto one another like lusty animals, jumping at each other again and again, and growl. Those sounds rebounding in the night air across spikes of red ginger and white Plumeria blossoms, hot humidity cooling us as we made love in its breeze.

I can see us lying there on that white eyelet spread. Black silk shirt opened out onto white eyelet cloth. How she'd slip it on button-by-button and lick me with her tongue as I undid each. Red palm leaves the shades of inner lips pulsating against vaginal walls. Wooden pineapples framing us along the bed. Behind us lay the blackness of the night. The two of us wrapped together in darkness as pink palm leaves enfold lovers inside a silk Hawaiian shirt.

FOR TANGERINES

She'd stride that tree,
sure-footed girl-boy.
Pulling until flesh
released stem from tree.
And climb back down
full cupped hands
filled with fruit.

One-by-one she sectioned tangerines
upon white sheets
of Belgian lace.
In bed when she fed me tangerines
with her tongue,
enticement lingered
along the breast.

Nibbling back
at morsels of skin,
she'd wait as love's fruit
dropped into her hands.

Ah, to be licked with
the juice of tangerines.
And after, make love
to quench the thirst.

MUSINGS ON CLAY

I did not know the sculptures living in her room.
Strange how she molded those pieces of life,
primal forces, fixed, yet alive.
Surrounding all this, there were her hands.

She molded pieces of life,
saucy dancers, voluptuous women,
mothers and babes.
With her hands,
she mused on women far into the night.

Sensuous dancers, voluptuous women,
mothers and babes,
limbs curving upwards encircling life's dance.
How she loved women far into the night.
Caressing, carving, and casting her clay.

CLATTER

I know he damaged you,
I could say nothing at the time.
Never the child he wanted you to be,
his yell at you louder than his soft speak to me.

I could say nothing at the time.
I, myself, silent in the midst of the din.
His yell at you louder than his soft speak to me.
We tasted our fear as it hung in that room.

I, myself, silent in the midst of the din.
The clatter of silver along untouched plates.
We tasted our fear as it hung in that room,
sat frozen as his words tormented the air.

The clatter of silver along untouched plates,
never the child he wanted you to be.
I, myself, silent in the midst of the din.
I know he damaged you.

A MOTHER'S LOVE

I know my mother loved me when I was a child.
Stories read together while seated on the couch.
Where did I go wrong, she cried when I said I loved a woman.
And pushed me away, just outside of her heart.

Stories read together while sitting on the couch.
Humming Irish lullabies she touched my fingers to roses and lace.
And pushed me away, just outside of her heart.
Sad, how we never found the way back.

Humming Irish lullabies she touched my fingers to roses and lace.
A mother's wish for this girl child of her born.
Sad, how we never found our way back.
Do children ever grow up as planned?

A mother's wish for this girl child of her born.
Where did I go wrong, she cried when I said I was gay.
Humming Irish lullabies she touched my fingers to roses and lace.
I know my mother loved me when I was a child.

CONJURING THE ORB

In Dolly Brown's house,
across the street from ours
50s jazz hums
behind pages of *Howl* and *Ellery Queen*,
while on a black leather sofa
a turtle-necked young woman stretches long.

One day, Dolly reveals a shiny, black ball.
With a question about her boyfriend,
she turns the orb in her hand.
The ball foretells *As I see it, yes.*

She urges me, young friend,
Go on, you try.
Offers the sphere to me from her palm.
Hesitating, I ask
Will I get married? Live in Detroit?
Questions of the future
pondered by a child.

Magical, that world in which she and I exist.
Life's answers revealed,
behind inky blue clouds.

Dolly Brown in that long black dress,
extends an 8 Ball to me in her hand.
One day, they find her in the bathtub, dead.
"A suicide," I hear my mother explain.
As if I understand death at 10.
For me, one day, Dolly Brown just isn't there.
I don't cross the street to her house anymore,
talk of futures and fortunes, or listen to jazz.

And the 8 ball?
It holds magical unworldliness,
to this day.
That shiny orb.
That slick, black ball.

SHINY SHOES

You were poor then.
Pennies fought for bought the heel of bread,
a few more, sandwich meat.
One pair of shoes, one black suit split between two.
Welfare woman knocking on the door,
always that fear she'd take away home.

When your mother's heart gave out,
they put her in an asylum.
In Detroit, they'd lock away the poor
like numbered people penned in camps.
Kept her there until she almost died.
Gave her back to you, broken.

TB left you upon Northville's bed,
Single rose stems
remembered each one as they died.
Somehow, through those youthful days,
you survived.

From all that you taught us,
"You have to keep on."
"You kids don't know what it was like," you'd say.
We didn't want to hear
your stories of how it was.
We were young then.
Born from newer cloth,
walked in shinier shoes.

THE OBJECTS I KEEP

I have their things in my drawer: rings and coins,
watches that once ticked with hands that spun round,
masonic rings that slid on fingers, inscribed;
powderless compacts topped by needlepoint scenes,
turquoise wedding earrings, bracelets of beads.

They are dead, but their stories
still float about in dreams.
A paleontologist,
I scratch memory from bone.

Grandma's dresser next to mine
in the same bedroom.
I remember opening her drawer,
fingering each piece secreted inside:
a black-jeweled star that hung on a chain,
silver filigree ring set inside a box.

That necklace of pearls that lay
in grandma's drawer,
how it reclined, satin-cushioned,
in a blue velvet case.
She wore it on those few special days,
though no pictures I have
show off the white orbs.

I do not remember taking scissors in hand,
nor do I recall putting fingers
inside the loops,
nor the clip of tin blades
as they slid between knots.

I did not open the drawer,
remove the case. Not my hands.
It was not I cutting through cord.

Grandma at the sink,
chops dinner vegetables along the old wooden board
holds up the knuckle she's cut with that knife,
her finger, the hand, the blood.
My mother wraps a cloth around the place
where the knife has cut.

A child is cutting a cord, separating each bead
from its place in a chain.
One-between-one, she severs the knots.
I stood silent when mother asked if it was I.
She couldn't understand why I'd cut that rope.

They are dead: Mother, Father, Grandmother.
I still have their things:
pearls I've hung around my neck,
Mother's gold pin on my jacket lapel,
silent watches in a silver tray.
The knife in my kitchen drawer, its serrated edge.

FLOWERS OF YOUTH

Somewhere in the middle of the night,
even though I try to
chase away dreams,
the stories as we left them
hang alive in the air.

In that city exist the ghosts of my dead.
There, where shadows drift on air,
people, once family,
appear again, alive.
Table set with china cups, crystal bowls.
Chairs covered in white damask and cerise-colored silk.

In that city of memory the words speak again.
The "you shouldn'ts" and "we don'ts"
mother taught when I was small.
Feelings girls shouldn't have,
red dresses good girls shouldn't wear.
Folding towels in threes, clothespinning sheets on the line.
Tables and chairs, linens and dough.
In that city endure the ghosts of my dead.

In that city of memory my father returns,
slams the front door and yells about work that day.
My aproned grandmother washes dishes
silently at the sink,
and wipes shaking wet hands along
a worn, flowered cloth.
While I twirl in the yard
amidst the lilacs of youth.

MARY MERIAM

COOL AND STABLE

MARY MERIAM is the editor of *Lavender Review* and the author of two poetry chapbooks, *The Countess of Flatbroke* and *The Poet's Zodiac*. The poems published here have previously appeared in Ali Liebegott's *Faggot Dinosaur*, *Alimentum*, *Sixty-Six: The Journal of Sonnet Studies*, *Horizon Review*, *Phati'tude*, *OCHO*, *Chiron Review*, *Rhythm Poetry Magazine*, and *Light Quarterly*.

http://lavrev.net

BAPTIST FAGGOT DINOSAUR

I'm at pump ten trying to sound rational in my mind. What is this gas, dinosaur bones? Then a siren, and since this is Arkansas, I hear a cop screaming faggots. Yes, I think gas comes from Earth, and that's where dinosaur bones are piled. They had to die somewhere, right? There must be tons of bones and dinosaur teeth. A van of baptists from Oklahoma stops at pump nine. They're from Earth too. I think Earth is made of dinosaurs, which were almost as big as Earth. One foot was like as big as Hawaii. They hopped around from Hawaii to Alaska to Manhattan. Continental drifts and divides meant nothing to them.

FARMER'S MARKET

watermelon: I was pretty once in an androgynous way
zucchini: now I am too old to be looked at by anyone
carrots: man or woman
cantaloupe: I shall not reveal my name or age
okra: if you saw me at the farmer's market
tomatoes: I would not be standing behind a table
onions: laden with tomatoes, onions
garlic: I would be carrying brown paper bags
yellow squash: filling them up
basil: I would not be the teenage boy
scallions: holding his father's arm
lettuce: legs strangely twisted
string beans: who walks with more vertical than horizontal
beets: movement, as if each step requires
eggplant: a leap into the air and the most intense concentration
radish: I am able to climb the staircase two steps at a time
sweet pepper: and climb the staircase seventy times
peaches: until sweat drips like blood
blackberries: my legs marble pillars
turnip: my vanity strong as my marble legs so that
parsley: I quickly forget the boy's twisted legs
cucumber: and his pain

MELON BALLS

What do I know of sex in my seclusion,
the big black bull outside the hot barbed wire,
the female rancher's sweat in the confusion,
for all I know, the bad bull's balls on fire?
I'm most familiar with my quiet table,
with casseroles, with roasted nuts and seeds,
with stewing beans, with salads cool and stable,
with satisfying simple daily needs.
A smooth-skinned melon? Yes, it fits my hands.
I feel the melon's soft warm weight and think
of her. A lizard nods. He understands?
I rinse the melon in the kitchen sink
and try to let my thoughts run down the drain.
The absence of her pleasure is my pain.

AN ENTERING

I am asleep on my city's dead street,
when you take my hand, and then we are walking;
there is silence, but I can feel your hand talking,
pulling me deeper into your warm, sweet
language, speaking to me, with a teacher's eloquence,
of your need, which is beginning to dawn on me
in the dark theater, where no one can see
the tutorial of your kisses, which are kindling the sense
of warmer and closer things yet to be known—
how could I then awaken, hideous, alone?

PORTRAIT OF A WOMAN REVEALING HER BREASTS

Sensing Tintoretto's brushes
on her breasts, tender, luscious,
she looks away and faintly blushes.

Can we understand the deal
she made to model and reveal?
Was it for love? Oh, let me feel

this love, then let my fingers slide
along each folded, flowing side
of parted dress and salty tide,

until I touch her strands of pearls.
Now tickled by her auburn curls
and wavy locks, her image twirls

an ocean where I cannot swim
and flailing, drown. Here on the slim
shore of sound, I sigh and limn.

HOT SPELL

This sonnet holds the hope of something hot:
a summer night with soft cicada din,
a sultry rush of fingers on the skin,
a tender lightning bolt that hits the spot.

Or in the city, ripe with heat and rot,
a staircase to a loft where we begin
a strip-down to the hardest core within,
a culture shock, the climax of the plot.

This sonnet drops my hand and doesn't care
that here I lie alone, again, in bed,
the chilly springtime flooding me with pain.
As if I need the sonnet to explain
a couplet rhymes, a couplet is a pair,
my sweat is rain, the heat is in my head.

ORPHIC CHANT

Let singer seek the way to hell,
and bring her back, and bring her back.
Let singer sound the hole of black,
and make her well, and make her well.
Let singer charm the deadly dell,
for knick the singer has a knack.
Let singer seek the way to hell,
and bring her back, and bring her back.
Let singer strike the silver bell.
Let singer ride the railroad track.
Let singer face the devil pack.
Let singer seek the way to hell,
and bring her back, and bring her back.

EAU SAUVAGE

Two windows weeping lilac curtains, sheer
and long, and lilac bushes perfume air
from snowy peaks. A quiet room, austere.
A mattress on the floor, a desk and chair.

The disco dancers throbbing in the dark,
drinking and drunk. Speed shots of burning light.
I go there. Why then does this woman park
herself in front of me and break the night?

Her eau sauvage for men. Her downcast eyes.
Her short black hair. *Intoxicate my mind,
Professor. Say your body tells no lies.
Loosen your full white bosom from its bind.*

At last seduced, I kiss her on the lips.
Again, again, the driving downbeat whips.

WHEN I MEET HER BY THE SEASHORE

I shall
untwine her time
unravel her travel
undo her mood
unfasten her battens
unmesh her dress
unbutton her bubbles
unleash her fresh.

And then I shall
unwind her behind
uncouple her trouble
unearth her worth
unstaple her paper
unzip her yip
unbuckle her tickle
untuck her lush.

MY RHONA

Ah yes, I scrutinized *The Art of Meeting
Women*, and fell for Rhona Sacks, her eyes,
her friendly smile, her hand held out in greeting,
her quick chit-chat. My Rhona is so wise!
I'd like to ask her, "Hey, what happens if
I'm not afraid, I'm not a slob, I say
hello, I'm cheery, kind, and not too stiff,
but she just doesn't care?" "Well then, don't stay,"
my Rhona pithily advises, "Move."
Helpfully, my Rhona urges lots
of get up, go, and find another groove.
"And if I'm stuck in her hard-hearted plots?"
"Break free," my Rhona counsels, "and be true
to the Rhona that I introduced you to."

MAUREEN SEATON

LOUD AS CHILDBIRTH

MAUREEN SEATON has authored fourteen poetry collections, both solo and collaborative, including her latest, *Genetics* (Jackleg Press). She is a two-time Lambda Award winner—for a memoir, *Sex Talks to Girls* (University of Wisconsin Press, 2008, The Living Out Series), and for *Furious Cooking* (University of Iowa Press, 1996). Her other awards include the Publishing Triangle's Audre Lorde Award, the Eighth Mountain Poetry Prize, the Society of Midland Authors Award, the Pushcart, and an NEA. Poems included here have previously appeared in *Pank, Chicago Review, River Oak Review, Ploughshares, Poetry East, Portraits of Love: Lesbians Writing About Love, Bathos Journal,* and *The Gay & Lesbian Review Worldwide.*

www.maureenseaton.com

WHEN I WAS BI(NARY)

I contrasted nicely with *unary,*
ternary, quarternary, and so on.
In this way, I functioned hypothetically

and trouble-free as a pair of bosons,
which, we know, will happily occupy
one quantum state, unlike two fermions.

Explosive, I fissioned and coded. My
planetary bodies orbited themselves
like a bi-asteroid, a bi-star (blue/white),

bi-nomials, and two cute daughter cells
that grew up opposite each other
and occasionally met in the middle

like lips. Sometimes I was a multiplier
in a two-based number system, enjoying
the way my human fingers desired

nothing more than the gratifying
mathematics of acey-deucey, ac/
dc, options flowing, always showing

off—like a superheroine or a tree.
For fun, I smote the rap of wishy-washy
and plucked the euphoric luck of binary.

REVELATION

So no one would dispute him, he said "historically"
empires have collapsed, folded, fallen, in other words

ceased to exist entirely at the precise moment
homosexuals walked openly in the public domain.

You mean (she said) that Gregg and Rick discussing rings
on Foster and Clark outside the Middle Eastern store

where we get great falafel are as powerful as the Ice Age?
That Valerie and Erica and Vanessa and Sue gobbling

plantanos and curried goat and collard greens and fried
chicken at the Tropical Oasis near Lake Michigan

are a twentieth century equivalent to the flood? They're
Horsewomen of the Apocalypse, four of the seven bowls of plagues?

His polemic went on logically (he hated Seuss) and soon
she was fitting her closet with bidet and microwave,

her dearest necessities, and he was driving to Little Village
for trysts with a masseur named Fred whose working name

was *Las Manos*, denying that either of them was acting queerly.
Off they went disguised as straight to a disguised B&B where

couples took off their clothes and practiced the cult
of swinging, with others, for others, on others, or around

others, the option she chose because she was unable to break free
from the habit of wholesomeness freckles automatically bequeath.

Thus time went on, she coveting girls, he coveting boys,
and on the seventh day they had a vision.

There they were on the Loyola Park Beach like Kiefer Sutherland
in *Flatliners* about to comment flatly and irrevocably that indeed

this is a good day to die when they heard the sound of a ridiculous
number of angels, *ten thousand times ten thousand of them...*

...all the living things in creation–everything
that lives in the air, and on the ground, and under the ground,

and in the sea, crying. And the animals said "Amen."
And the elders from Edgewater prostrated themselves on benches

and slept off decades as they longed to do. And they did.
It was the prelude to the prelude to the great day that followed

when the seventh angel blew her trumpet and the queers came out,
every one, loud as childbirth, and the world, as we knew it, died.

THE STRANGE

Be mindful on those rain-spent days when litter pools around your toes
and falcons beckon. You'll be walking with your girlfriend in hetero-

steeped Harlem, NY, where the soul-food restaurant lady will pour salt
on your collard greens like a layer of thin ice, your nice girlfriend

will produce a small knife and threaten several souls in said restaurant—
you have a GIRLFRIEND, sweet Jesus, and while she's

navigating perfect sex with you behind bars that keep you trapped yet safe
from the rest of New Yorkers, she couldn't possibly guess this is not

your true life. On the #3 home, this is not you. At Danny's Chicken:
someone else. Driving the 18-foot Ryder with clutch and choke, the feet

that used to be yours don't even touch the floor—Jersey, Pennsylvania,
Ohio, Indiana—ink-armed truckers signaling you to switch lanes

as if you belong. Be aware that on cloudless days of no obvious redemption
you'll be peddling books sincerely in the midst of a tornado watch,

cotton puffs blowing like snowy shrapnel around the Midwest sky, now
you're IN THE MIDWEST, for godsake, and no one knows this is not

your normal M.O. Once you were snug between a father and a mother.
You crossed your feet like a ballerina. On Halloween you dressed up

in a pink tulle shirt and a crown made of foil. You had no idea
how much a twelve-year-old could bleed, how empty you could become

in one rum-soaked night. There are days to watch out for—the non-charmed,
the mammoth mundane—when the bells at Queen of Angels toll *Mary,*

we crown thee with blossoms and you wake beside a woman in Chicago.

THE CHURCH OF GOD IN CHRIST ON THE HILL

There's nothing more seductive than the basement
of this gated and clapboard building

in Bed-Stuy, Brooklyn, on a Sunday afternoon when
Sister Walker's got the turkey wings

and the fried chicken and the baked
macaroni and the green beans and candied yams

simmering on every burner in the tiny kitchen
while upstairs all the brothers sing

in witness, hallelujah, and the sisters jog around the church
because their knees don't have arthritis today

and their blood pressure is not up,
and the children sleep on soft cushions,

Sunday clothes pressed and red
and pink and Pastor's black robes flow

like the Nile with the baby Moses directly
to the arms of God. No one cares

Jesus and I are white. That I sit in my pew
one big blush of praise at the trumpets and the drums

and the tambourines in this Baptist orgy of the soul.
No one cares because THEY KNOW HOW TO WAIT.

"You can get by," Pastor Dallas says, "But, honey,
you can't get away." Talking about back-sliders,

talking about lapses of faith, infidelity,
homosexuality, God waiting patiently for revenge. I'm

thinking about the 'coon man out on the street
with those three dead-as-doornail raccoons

he climbed down the sewer to shoot last night
at the crest of his Bacardi high. I'm thinking

about Satan. And my Catholic upbringing
wafts around me like Sister Walker's chicken. As if

I've fasted since midnight, as if I'm eight years old
and Pastor says; "You have to make an *arrangement*

with God." Leaving out the *g* so I picture myself
arraigned before Jesus and Mary and the Twelve who

never had sex again after they heard the Good News. Those
raccoons laid out on the sidewalk

so quiet and guilty. Lori and I marching
toward the Church of God in Christ on the Hill

with our interracial fallen-away selves. As if
we're standing in the courtroom of God

and we're swaying from the turkey wings and yams
and Pastor Dallas yelling about the prodigal son,

how the father said: "Kill the fatted calf—
Don't eat that slop the pigs eat!"

And Lori says she's so hungry she could eat that slop,
and her grandmother says:

"Don't leave until after the altar call, girls."
But we do, walking down that aisle

as if we were holy. Those raccoons
baking in the sun on Rochester, 'coon man

drinking his first Sunday rum. All over
Bed-Stuy there's religion and sin,

homos and straight people, Pastor and 'coon man,
everyone getting mixed up in the witnessing

and the hunger and everyone
floating down the Nile toward the Pharaoh

or salvation.

THE MALL

On line at Manchu Wok, he orders two #3 combinations:
broccoli and beef, chop suey, fried rice, and maneuvers

through shoppers at packed tables to a sorrowful wife who
pokes at her #3 food with a fork, barely glancing up. He

can't take his eyes off you. Why? No special reason I can see
except you're still butch as the day I met you.

We're in line for #4's: chop suey, fried rice, chicken balls,
and you can't seem to do a damned thing right.

He's glaring and we order and pay and eat and you're
talking: What presents are left to buy the kids,

how do I like the chicken balls, any more soy sauce?
And the mall begins to switch, takes on a certain

twenty-yards-of-dusty-street-in-the-wild-west look
and he's got a shotgun pointed at your back. He's

growing taller, and all the shoppers are mean with hunger.
You have no idea you're about to die. "Let's

ride," I say and gather up coats and bags and eggrolls.
And before your lips can form a "What the...," we're

cowboys bolting out of town on slippery horses. "I love you,"
I shout to the streak of light I know is you beside me

PASSING

The waitress at Baker's Square glides toward us like a boat,
like a big mother, a head nurse, and writes down "pie."

When she calls you "Sir," we know we've got it made.
Ha ha ha. We do this a long time. *Ha.*

We feel high after the wisecracks on Clark,
the narrowed eyes of young men on Estes, their threats

to our anatomy, two women with the nerve to come bi-racial.
"Take my hand," you say, reveling so hard

in our sudden status of semi-legitimate Americans
you want to exploit every precious convention.

We analyze you: Slick-backed, ponytailed hair, two earrings,
soft red shirt. Must be the shoes, the tie, the way

your eyebrow slides up as I slide my ass into the booth,
the way you defer to me as if I were royalty.

"You look like a woman to me," I whisper, so innocent
the ice cream on my apple pie melts, so silky

your biceps twitch beneath your shirt. "Kiss me," you say.
And I do. Leaning across coffee like any ordinary female,

sanctioned and smug to my toes with public approval,
the tip of my tongue a secret between us.

SEX TALKS WITH GIRLS

When sleeping in the same bed with another girl, old or young, avoid 'snuggling up',
close together...and, after going to bed, if you are sleeping alone or with others, just
bear in mind that beds are sleeping places. When you go to bed, go to sleep just as
quickly as you can.

—*Ten Sex Talks to Girls*, Irving D. Steinhardt (*1914*)

Girls may appear innocent, even girls
whose breasts develop early and who
calmly wait for their body to grow hair
down there and under here, places no girl
should ever look. Turn your thoughts to creweling
tablecloths. Cook a moist turkey, tat
a pillowcase. There is no better way
through puberty than the fine art of Home
Economics. Cupcakes are a great dis-
traction from awkward sexual urges.

Remember that God made Adam, and Eve
fell for a viper while our first man
stood by munching a Macintosh. Pity
boys—they aren't equipped to compete with snakes.
For instance, where would we be if Snow White
had settled for wildlife? Fairy tales are great
guides for living. Like the Lives of the Saints.
Saints had their hands cut off rather than sin.
Don't waste your time on girls. It's like kissing
a mirror or rubbing against a stuffed cat.

It is never okay to hug a girl
who looks like James Dean. If you're unable
to stop yourself, invoke the name of your
patron saint, and think about martyrs. If
it's Joan, ask her to guide you through the fire
of your formative years. She herself died
too young to think about sex in her man-
ly clothes with her sword and her armor suit.
But remember: They burned her alive for her-
esy. (Even now, you've got to wonder.)

To summarize: Sleep quickly and alone.
Stay away from snakes, Joan of Arc, James Dean
flicks, and women's sports. Cook furiously
to appease hormones. Do not trust flowers.
Consider the seaside a possible
temptation. When developing a crush,
check for a *real* penis and stop yourself
if you don't see a white horse. Everything
should be Disney or saintly. Under no
circumstances should there be chemistry.

SALLY FIELD

If I could be any actor it would be Sally Field. If I could sleep with
any actor it would be Queen Latifah. Field reminds me a little of me
if I weren't so phobic about flying. Latifah, you might say, has
become a famous femme in recent years—if you judge by the makeup
and the glossy magazine spreads. Still, the way she rapped in the old
days...and that *Set It Off* scene. The thing I like about Field is her
seamless approach to her life and work. Plus she's a mom and she
says censorable things. I like that she loved two men in *Norma Rae*.
I've had trouble myself loving just one person over the years. I could
easily have three lovers at a time like a Mormon or a beach cat.
Latifah reminds me of the night one of my lovers dressed up as a
femme fatale and sang me a torch song. Not all butches can do that.
Some look like drag queens when they put on femme clothes. Even
with a construction hat and steel-toed boots I femme myself out.
That's where Sally Field and I have something else in common.
Cowboy boots just make us look cuter.

FOUND LITURGY (REDUX)

If I'd married the gentle young man with the hair lip instead
of the vicarious bohemian with the propensity for large butts

and rosy knee caps, I'd have strolled along in sublime serenity
instead of rumbling through my maiden phase like the Howard

bearing down on North and Clybourn, that turn in the tracks
where the conductor says *Whee* and we're expected, faithful

congregation, to lean left and continue whatever religious rites
we practice on subways: prayer beads, bible, clawing, dreaming.

One day I might have departed for a bluer warmer place:
the Keys! pointing to the ocean like fingers of a kind country.

Moved away from this country altogether, to Mojacar, Spain,
with its nude beach, its *playa naturista*, and fat buttery

mujeres who laugh (*ha!*) at the scrawny models in *Cosmopolitan*
while their *hombres* remember the sweet fucking of the night before.

Even the thought—goofy, apocryphal—that had I been able to choose
which body I'd prefer to inhabit as I waited in the universe

I'd have chosen soprano, green thumb, old wealth, rock star.
The thought that someday we will all live together on the head of a pin

or fly to the uninhabitable moons of Jupiter to experience options
of antioxidants and uninhibited youth. Everything I've ever thought,

I *had* to think, think of it, every synapse, every charged neuron
tingling along its DNA, every scarlet image, every note I've plucked

in *A* or *D* or *B*: predestined as the teetering ascendancy of America.
I love the word *kismet*. I love throwing it into the atmosphere

to see what it brings back. Once it brought back a woman who landed
in my lap in the key of G, a key I instantly recognized and sang:

Melancholy Baby, Sweet Adeline, O Holy Holy Night.

JAN STECKEL

LITTLE WHIMPERS

JAN STECKEL is a physician who retired early, a bisexual and disability rights activist, and a poet and writer. Her *Mixing Tracks* (Gertrude Press, 2009) won the Gertrude Press fiction chapbook award for LGBT writers. Her chapbook *The Underwater Hospital* (Zeitgeist Press, 2006) won a Rainbow Award for lesbian and bisexual poetry. Her writing has appeared in *Scholastic Magazine*, *Yale Medicine*, *Bellevue Literary Review*, *Harrington Lesbian Literary Quarterly*, *Anything That Moves*, and elsewhere. She has been nominated twice for a Pushcart Prize. Her first full-length poetry book, *The Horizontal Poet*, is available from Zeitgeist Press.

www.jansteckel.com

BRINGING

First girl I kissed.
You lured me to the squat you shared
with that "old man":
only middle-aged as I am now.
TV on, him in the La-Z-Boy.
A room divided in two by a bookcase.
We huddled on the other side.
"He can't see through," you whispered.
He could, though. I saw him seeing.
You dug out a slightly crushed joint,
shared it as promised. Wound
your hand in my neck-nape's hair,
nibbled my throat. Pot
swept me into the you-ness of you,
your soft lips, little whimpers.
I feared I'd get you thrown
onto the street again,
until it dawned on me
he wasn't letting you
bring me home.
You were letting him
watch you
bring me off.

DUCK, DUCK, GOOSED

Devil ducky sits impaled on a shower caddy's
rubber-coated wire. Ducky's getting goosed.
He's a butt-fucked glow-in-the-dark divine ducky.
At two a.m. he shines only in the corner of the eye.
Look straight at him, and he'll disappear in the dark.

I lie on the couch with a giant peppermint
stick up my skirt. I'm getting goosed.
I'm a peppermint-goosed glow-in-the-light diva.
At party time, I'll shine in the eye's corner.
Look straight at me. I'll match the décor.

My husband sits impaled on an unrealistically
large dildo. He's greased up, goosed but good.
He's my butt-fucked glow-in-the-dark divine darling.
At two a.m. he shines only in the corner of my mind.
Look into his eyes, and he'll disappear in the dark.

A LIFE AS BRIGHT AS IT WAS SHORT

I once knew a drag queen named Deshabille,
who sang "I Believe in Miracles." "Look out!"
she'd cry when the conversation waxed dull,
"I've got a pair of tweezers, and I know
how to use 'em!" She was as true
a goddess as any womon-born-womon.
She liked to discourse lovingly in French
about the sexual habits of snails, and finally wrote
a lengthy treatise entitled "Les Amours des limaçons"
on the "double embrassement de ces hermaphrodites."
Once that great work was finished, so was she.
On her deathbed she whispered "Never forget
to stop and smell the plastic corks." Then,
like a champagne bubble, she was—gone.

CARNAL BARKER

Love lights a cigarette.
Cherub cheeks glow in the fag-end's sparkle.
Venus better keep her fly-trap shut.
There's none here but hole-lickers,
cherry-red rimmers, and ass-kissing sinners.
A little bird told me, a faygele whispered:
Be she never so buxom
there's no place like home base,
no whole-heart like my hole, my heart.
So shut your pie-hole and give us a kiss,
you quick-thinking, piss-drinking
son of a cunt. Come on a hunt with me:
Find me one honest man
in the stews, moist and used,
and I'll screw the whole lot of you.
I know how you like it
you dyke-fucking piker. Strike words
from the record like sparks from a flint.
Dumb bint. You know you like it
so climb on my spike, have a ride, yes, You
with your girlfriend's red satin undies on.
Every man has his muse.
Grab your fountain pen, trash-talker,
fashion me a crash course in liberty:
one good poem before I die.
That's all I need to blow this popsicle stand.
One jay away from the world's memory.
Arm me with lexicons, pyrotechnicians.
Mexicans'll breed you out of English-only
you great Anglo-Saxon hussy. So buss me.
Kyrie eleison. Don't let me put a crimp
in your shrimping, you fast-dying fetishists.
Boot-licking fish-kissers. What Brueghel nightmare
gave rise to you here? A Bosch of a boot-master:
Shine 'em up bright girl!
Make your Nazi mama proud.
Plenty of time to wind
your own damned shroud.
Unwind a little. Just relax.
It will be over soon.

PREVENTATIVE DENTISTRY

On my world, women's mouths are also their vaginas.
Because they have to give birth through their mouths,
all their teeth are prophylactically removed.

The Knocking Out of Teeth used to be done
at the age of first menses as a coming-of-age rite.

Girls were grouped in age cohorts for their instruction
on how not to cry out when the blows came,
how to stanch the blood afterward
and pack their mouths with cotton.

In our modern age, this barbarism has disappeared
from all but the most isolated reaches of the planet.

Now girls have their teeth extracted under anesthesia,
once their jaws have stopped growing
(as determined by their dentists).

They are fitted with dentures, taught by their mothers
how to cement the false teeth in, how to clean them,
and when it is and isn't appropriate to remove them.

Once in a while a pervert molests a dentate girl.
Such men are judged mentally ill,
as they risk the integrity of their penises
by inserting them into such a dangerous place.

The victim's dentist has to subject the girl
to an oral exam so invasive
it feels like a second rape.

The feminists of your world object to our customs,
but their attempts to censure us are insensitive
and the worst kind of cultural imperialism.

You don't hear us railing in the United Planets
about all the obscene things
you let your women put into their mouths.

BIL DONOVAN

VESSEL REFLECTION

BIL DONOVAN is an artist, fashion illustrator, and educator. His artistic journey began in his birthplace of South Philadelphia where for two years he attended evening classes at The Art Institute of Philadelphia. A desire to pursue a career in fashion illustration initiated a move to New York and a degree in Illustration from The Fashion Institute of Technology. He has studied at The Art Students League, Parsons, and The School of Visual Arts, where he earned a BFA. Fulfilling a lifelong dream, he embarked on a three-month sojourn to Europe to experience life, art, and opportunity. Three months evolved into seven years of living and working in Milan and Paris. Donovan credits this invaluable experience in shaping his sensibility and style and returned home to New York to establish a working relationship with the advertising, beauty, editorial, and fashion markets. Bil currently resides in the East Village in New York City and works from his creative utopia, a studio in Tribeca.

bildonovan.com

ALSO FROM SIBLING RIVALRY PRESS

For the Comfort of Automated Phrases by Jane Cassady is a bottle of wine on a blanket in the park. It's a night on the couch with your girlfriend, your boyfriend—or *both* of them. It's making soup for a friend with a sick child. It's the beautiful unpretentious. At its heart, this is a book of love poems written starry-eyed to board games and geography, to pop culture and pop music, to nephews and cats and cities and singers. Cassady's full-length debut is the poetic equivalent of mix tape—one you'll keep rewinding and replaying—one that could easily be the soundtrack to your life.

www.siblingrivalrypress.com

CPSIA information can be obtained at www.ICGtesting.com
Printed in the USA
BVOW070349121012
302805BV00001B/9/P